A FURTHER LOOK AT SOUTHAMPTON'S QUAYSIDE RAILWAYS

Dave Marden

Kestrel Railway Books
PO Box 269
SOUTHAMPTON
SO30 4XR

www.kestrelrailwaybooks.co.uk

Printed by the Amadeus Press.

ISBN 978-1-905505-12-8

To Jen, for all her patience - while I've been losing mine.

Front cover: Esso Hunslet No 8999/1981 at work on the exchange sidings at the old Fawley S.R. station on 15ᵗʰ April 2008. (Author)

Back cover, top: A trio of Ruston shunters (07001/02/13) crawls past the Central Road police offices in the Eastern Docks on 17ᵗʰ August 1974. (Bert Moody)

Back cover, bottom left: Esso's GEU 0-4-4-0 loco No 20843 built 1949 pictured at Southampton Docks after arrival from New York on 3ʳᵈ January 1950 aboard the vessel "Vandalia". (Bert Moody Collection)

Back cover, bottom right: Passengers aboard the Hythe Pier Railway about to depart the landward terminal under the watchful eye of the ferry staff in 1955. (Roger Holmes)

Contents

Introduction and Acknowledgments

This second book on Southampton's industrial and minor railways is intended as both sequel and companion to my previous volume, *Southampton's Quayside Steam,* which focussed exclusively on the steam shunting locomotives within the confines of the city's docks, piers and river wharves. The precept being to give concise histories of those lines and the locomotives that served on them.

In *A Further Look at Southampton's Quayside Railways*, I have maintained the same formula in respect of locally based shunters, and included locations slightly further afield, although still within the Southampton area. I have also featured non-steam traction and narrow gauge lines, and while some of the subjects might be a little removed from the more recognisable classes of locomotive, their diversity of design and employment makes them all the more interesting. All locomotives are of standard gauge unless otherwise indicated.

I've also used a little "author's licence" to include some railways that, while not exactly on the quayside, were sufficiently near to the water's edge to justify inclusion. The chapters on Woolston Tip, Millbrook Foundry and the Hythe Rubber Works all fall into that category and, in their own way, help to complete the local picture. For a similar reason I have included the railway at Netley Hospital; although this never had its own dedicated locomotives, its importance in local history is too great to be omitted.

Some of the lines previously covered have been revisited, in particular those where steam power was superseded by diesel, and in other cases to include additional photographs that were omitted through lack of space first time around. In such instances I have not repeated the earlier extensive histories of the lines and locomotives, but instead provided brief overviews and outline details for the sake of familiarisation.

Throughout this volume there are numerous references to locomotives built by the Motor Rail Company under the name of Simplex. These engines, generally referred to as "tractors", were once commonplace on countless narrow gauge (and some standard gauge) railways where the machines gave immeasurable service and reliability over many decades.

Most of the early examples were provided for the Ministry of Munitions' War Department Light Railway (WDLR) for use in the WWI battle zones, where their operations on light railways were less conspicuous than steam locomotives. Depending on their usage, models were constructed as either Open, Protected or Armoured types according to their proximity to enemy action. When hostilities ceased, huge numbers of these machines were sold off to civilian and industrial firms throughout Britain and abroad, many having been stockpiled and never employed.

The locos came in various designs and engine sizes, but in general terms were predominantly of 2 ft gauge with 1ft 6in wheels and a 3ft 4in wheelbase, and these dimensions should be regarded unless otherwise indicated. Over the ensuing years, many examples have been rebuilt and renumbered, whilst being converted from the original petrol to diesel driven engines, which became the norm after 1930.

It is hoped that the two volumes will together present a useful and informative guide to the railways and locomotives that have graced Southampton's watersides – not always attractive but certainly honest and valued workhorses that played such an important role in the city's industrial development and history.

As before, I am indebted to fellow members of both the Industrial Railway Society and the Industrial Locomotive Society whose personal assistance, published works and exhaustive records have been of immense help. Thanks must again be given to the willing and helpful staff at Southampton City Archive and once more to Mr. Bert Moody whose comprehensive knowledge of local history has often been called upon by this author. Also worthy of mention is the Kidderminster Railway Museum whose large photographic archive has been an invaluable source of illustrations, and their friendly cooperation is greatly appreciated.

Where known, sources of photographs are given due credit following reasonable efforts to establish their origin and to contact the photographer for permission of use. If I have inadvertently overlooked or accidentally infringed anyone's copyright, I offer my sincere apologies.

Reference must be made to the following works that have provided rich sources of information:

The Calshot and Fawley Narrow Gauge Railways by Frederick W. Cooper
Hythe Pier and Ferry - A History by Alan Titheridge
The Fawley Branch by J.R. Fairman
Netley Hospital and its Railways by J.R. Fairman
Locomotives of the Ministry of Defence by R.K. Hateley
War Department Locomotives by R. Tourret
Southampton's Railways by Bert Moody
Shipbuilding in Victorian Southampton by Adrian B. Rance
A Guide to Simplex NG Locomotives by D.R. Hall & J.A.S. Rowlands

Dave Marden 2009.

Southampton Docks 1842 – 1979

After its formation in 1842, Southampton Docks had employed many types and classes of steam locomotives, beginning in 1865 with an odd assortment of individual engines in the days of the Southampton Dock Company, continuing with the B4 Class of the LSWR, and afterwards the Southern Railway ownership saw the introduction of the USA tanks, followed by E1s and E2s in the BR era. These were occasionally supplemented by classes C14, D1 and latterly E4 until the final phase of railway operation under British Rail saw the arrival of diesel traction in 1962.

Left: Former Southampton Dock Company locomotive No 118 "Vulcan" between duties at Eastleigh on 9ᵗʰ April 1922.
(Author's Collection)

Below: "Ironside" was the last of the Dock Company locos and survived into BR days as No 30458. It is seen here at Guildford on 22ⁿᵈ September 1951.
(John A. Bailey/Bert Moody Collection)

The final phase of the docks steam era beckons as USA tank No 70 (later 30070) and crew pose for the camera at the Western Docks on 29th November 1950.
(Author's Collection)

Post WWII days at the Eastern Docks running shed where B4s "St Malo" and "Jersey" keep an eye on newcomer USA No 67. Soon, the elderly LSWR locos would be entirely replaced by the Yanks.
(Author's Collection)

The steam era at Southampton Docks is drawing to a close with assorted locos at the Eastern Docks running shed in the early 1960s. On the left E2 32104 is parked with USA 30069. 30062 is at the shed entrance while a visiting E4 stands in the background.
(Lens of Sutton Collection)

SOUTHAMPTON DOCKS 1842 – 1979

When steam's final days became numbered, as with previous administrations, a fleet of 14 locomotives was required and a class of specially designed 0-6-0 diesel electric shunters was purchased from Ruston & Hornsby at Lincoln, their main dimensions being:

Driving Wheels: 3ft 6ins
Wheelbase: 8ft 7.5ins
Engine: Paxman 275 hp
Weight: 42ton 18cwt
Fuel tank: 300gals

These locomotives were classified as BR 07 class and had a maximum speed of 20mph. Their original number series ran from D2985 to D2998 but this was amended to 07001 – 07014 under the TOPS scheme (Total Operation Processing System) in 1971 but not all received their new identities before disposal.

In comparison with their predecessors, their allocation to the docks was short-lived and by 1975 only five remained on regular duties (four being rostered at any one time). With the docks rail system having been largely abandoned by then, the remainder were moved on to other locations, put into storage, or sold to new owners. Today, half the class still survive – albeit in various states of preservation or decay. With the Rustons gone, the few occasional demands for rail operations were carried out by class 08 English Electric diesels, dispatched from Eastleigh, until 1979 when freight movements between the docks ceased after the rail link past the Town Quay was closed. The last of the line included No 08151 and No 08642. There is still rail access to both the Eastern and Western Docks, but movements are now worked by main line stock instead of docks based locomotives.

An 07 class Ruston Diesel with a train of empty coaches from Western Docks passes through the Eastern Docks Engineers yard in the mid 1960s. (Bert Moody Collection)

A cavalcade of past and present dock locos lines up against a backdrop of the SS Canberra at No 7 drydock in June 1962. From left to right are classes B4, USA, E2 and Ruston 07 diesel. These represented some 84 years of motive power in the port. (Author's Collection)

Final days – English Electric shunter No 08642 with a train of car transporters carrying vehicles for export at 40 Berth, Eastern Docks in 1979. (Bert Moody Collection)

BR Southampton Docks 0-6-0DE Ruston & Hornsby No 480686

Manufacturer:	Ruston & Hornsby Ltd
Built:	1962
Works number:	480686
Running numbers:	D2985, 07001 (both BR)
At the docks:	1962 – 1977

This was the first of the purpose-built R&H locos for Southampton Docks, arriving in June 1962, unceremoniously by road transport on a low loader. Based at the docks running shed, it remained in service there until June 1977 when it was placed in store at Eastleigh. It was sent for overhaul at Tilsley & Lovett Ltd, Trentham, Staffordshire in April 1978 and subsequently sold to Holderness Limeworks at Peak Dale in Derbyshire in the following month. After more than a decade of service there it was taken to the South Yorkshire Railway Preservation Society at Meadow Hall in Sheffield in June 1989. From there it went on hire to scrap merchants Mayer Parry at Snailwell in Suffolk from April 1993 until October 1997 before moving to its present home at the Barrow Hill Roundhouse Railway Centre in June 1999.

Southampton Docks shunter No D2985 with a train of containers passing Town Quay.
(Peter Saunders Collection)

BR Southampton Docks 0-6-0DE Ruston & Hornsby No 480687

Manufacturer:	Ruston & Hornsby Ltd
Built:	1962
Works number:	480687
Running numbers:	D2986, 07002 (both BR)
At the docks:	1962 – 1977

D2986 was one of the initial batch of purpose-built R&H locos that arrived in June 1962. Based at the docks running shed it remained in service there until June 1977 when it was placed in store at Eastleigh. From there it was sold, along with D2990, to Powell Duffryn Fuels at Coed Bach opencast disposal site at Kidwelly in April 1978, where it worked until being scrapped by T. Davies of Llanelli in September 1982.

Southampton Dock shunter No D2986 with a goods train passes SS Canberra in No 7 Drydock on 26th June 1962. (Peter Saunders Collection)

BR Southampton Docks 0-6-0DE Ruston & Hornsby No 480688

Manufacturer:	Ruston & Hornsby Ltd
Built:	1962
Works number:	480688
Running numbers:	D2987, 07003 (both BR)
At the docks:	1962 – 1976

One of the initial batch of purpose-built R&H docks locos, D2987 arrived in June 1962 and was based at the docks running shed where it remained until October 1976. It was then withdrawn from service at Eastleigh and sold on to R.E Trem at Finningly, Doncaster in March the following year. A move to British Industrial Sand at Oakamoor followed in October 1978 where this loco gave several more years service until being scrapped in June 1985.

BR Southampton Docks 0-6-0DE Ruston & Hornsby No 480689

Manufacturer:	Ruston & Hornsby Ltd
Built:	1962
Works number:	480689
Running numbers:	D2988 (BR)
At the docks:	1962 – 1973

Another of the first arrivals of purpose-built R&H docks shunters to appear at Southampton in June 1962. D2988 was also one of the first to be disposed of when withdrawn at BR's Eastleigh works in May 1973 and broken up there in November that year, never having had its TOPS number of 07004 applied.

Above: D2988 with sister engine D2987 alongside Southampton Western Docks Carriage Shed. (Jack Perry Archive Collection)

Right: D2987 at Southampton's Eastern Docks. (Jack Perry Archive Collection)

BR Southampton Docks 0-6-0DE Ruston & Hornsby No 480690

Manufacturer:	Ruston & Hornsby Ltd
Built:	1962
Works number:	480690
Running numbers:	D2989, 07005 (both BR), L106 (Resco)
At the docks:	1962 – 1977

The last of the initial batch of purpose-built R&H locos to arrive at Southampton Docks in June 1962. D2989 was also one of the final departures in July 1977. After withdrawal by BR it was sent for overhaul to Resco, Woolwich in June 1978 who allocated it their number L106. It was subsequently purchased by ICI at Wilton, Middlesbrough in July the following year (where it carried the name *Langbaurgh*) and was reunited there with sister engine D2995 in September 1980. In December 2000 it was moved to the Barrow Hill Railway and then on to the Battlefield Line at Shackerstone, Leicestershire in September 2003 where it resides in a dilapidated state, and such is its condition that it is unlikely to become operational again.

BR Southampton Docks 0-6-0DE Ruston & Hornsby No 480691

Manufacturer:	Ruston & Hornsby Ltd
Built:	1962
Works number:	480691
Running numbers:	D2990, 07006 (both BR)
At the docks:	1962 – 1977

Following the initial arrivals in June 1962, this loco was one of a pair (with D2991) of purpose built R&H shunters to arrive at Southampton Docks in the following month. D2990 was also one of the final departures in July 1977. After withdrawal by BR it was sold, together with D2986, to Powell Duffryn Fuels at the Coed Bach opencast disposal point in April 1978, where it worked until scrapped in October 1984.

D2990 pictured at Eastleigh. (Jack Perry Archive Collection)

D2989 enjoys a moment's rest between duties. (Author's Collection)

BR Southampton Docks 0-6-0DE Ruston & Hornsby No 480692

Manufacturer:	Ruston & Hornsby Ltd
Built:	1962
Works number:	480692
Running numbers:	D2991 (BR)
At the docks:	1962 – 1973

D2991 was one of the second wave of purpose-built shunters to arrive at Southampton Docks in July 1962. However, with three others of the 07 class its tenure was comparatively short lived when withdrawn from service in May 1973 never having been given its TOPS number (07007). Unlike many of its counterparts it survived the scrapyard by becoming used as a static generator at Eastleigh Railway Works. After being saved by the Eastleigh Railway Preservation Society, it has been employed by train refurbishment company Knights Rail Services at the works since March 2007.

D2991 at Eastleigh on 27th September 1992. (Jack Perry Archive Collection)

BR Southampton Docks 0-6-0DE Ruston & Hornsby No 480693

Manufacturer:	Ruston & Hornsby Ltd
Built:	1962
Works number:	480693
Running numbers:	D2992 (BR)
At the docks:	1962 – 1973

Another of the second wave of Ruston shunters to arrive at Southampton Docks in July 1962. D2992 never received its TOPS number (07008) before withdrawal in May 1973 and subsequent storage at Eastleigh works until scrapped in August 1976.

D2992 at Eastleigh Works in storage with an unidentified sister on 10th March 1974.
(Jack Perry Archive Collection)

BR Southampton Docks 0-6-0DE Ruston & Hornsby No 480694

Manufacturer:	Ruston & Hornsby Ltd
Built:	1962
Works number:	480694
Running numbers:	D2993, 07009 (both BR)
At the docks:	1962 – 1976

D2993 was the sole representative of the 07 class to arrive at Southampton Docks in August 1962. Having received its TOPS number of 07009 it continued in service there until October 1976 when, being surplus to requirements, it was sold by BR to Shipbreakers at Queenborough, Kent. In March 1977 was exported to Trieste, Italy, having been sold to the firm of Attilio Rossi in Rome, who employed it on track works until it was scrapped in May 1997.

BR Southampton Docks 0-6-0DE Ruston & Hornsby No 480695

Manufacturer:	Ruston & Hornsby Ltd
Built:	1962
Works number:	480695
Running numbers:	D2994, 07010 (both BR)
At the docks:	1962 – 1976

D2994, latterly 07010, arrived at Southampton Docks with sister loco D2995 in September 1962. After being withdrawn from service and stored at Eastleigh in October 1976, it was soon taken into preservation on the Mid-Hants Railway until transferred to the West Somerset Railway in 1978. It then moved on to the Avon Valley Railway in 1994, where it has had a major rebuild and is used primarily as a backup loco.

Above: 07010 negotiates the traffic at the approach to No 5 gate with a train of internal stock for the Western Docks on 18th July 1975. (Author)

Right: D2993 as 07009 at Southampton's Western Docks. (Author's Collection)

D2995 as 07011 with sister 07s at Southampton Western Docks Carriage Shed on 10th March 1974. (Jack Perry)

Class 07 No 2996 with a train heating boiler van in tow near the docks running shed on 19th June 1965.
(W. Potter/KRM Collection)

BR Southampton Docks 0-6-0DE Ruston & Hornsby No 480696

Manufacturer:	Ruston & Hornsby Ltd
Built:	1962
Works number:	480696
Running numbers:	D2995, 07011 (both BR), L104 (Resco)
At the docks:	1962 – 1977

D2995, latterly 07011, was the second of two Ruston shunters delivered to Southampton Docks by the makers in September 1962, the other being D2994. Its duties in the port lasted a little longer than those of the latter, when it was taken out of service in July 1977. Having been rebuilt by Resco at Woolwich in June 1978 it was allocated their number L104 and sent on hire to ICI at Billingham in March 1979, returning in November that year. Its period at ICI was obviously successful as they purchased the loco in September 1980 and employed it at their Wilton Works at Middlesbrough, where it carried the name *Cleveland* and renewed its partnership with sister engine D2989 for several more years. After a move to Hastings Diesels in May 1996 it found its way to the Kent & East Sussex Railway in 1998, before being privately preserved at Railway Engineering Ltd, Bridgemary, St. Leonards on Sea in July 2000.

BR Southampton Docks 0-6-0DE Ruston & Hornsby No 480697

Manufacturer:	Ruston & Hornsby Ltd
Built:	1962
Works number:	480697
Running numbers:	D2996, 07012 (both BR)
At the docks:	1962 – 1977

D2996 was delivered from R&H in October 1962, being the only 07 class shunter to arrive that month. After being renumbered 07012 it was one of the last to see service at the docks when withdrawn from service in July 1977. It was sold to Powell Duffryn Fuels at the Cmw Mawr Disposal Point at Tumble, Dyfed in April 1978, and by 1982 had moved to the company's Coed Bach Disposal site at Kidwelly. Having been purchased for preservation by the Harry Needle Railroad Co Ltd on Merseyside in 1992 it was moved to the South Yorkshire Railway Preservation Society at Meadowhall, Sheffield in December of that year. In June 2001 it was taken to the Lavender Line in East Sussex before transfer to its present home at the Barrow Hill Railway at Chesterfield in July 2006, where it is currently non-operational.

BR Southampton Docks 0-6-0DE Ruston & Hornsby No 480698

Manufacturer:	Ruston & Hornsby Ltd
Built:	1962
Works number:	480698
Running numbers:	D2997, 07013 (both BR), L101 (Resco)
At the docks:	1962 – 1977

This engine was one of a pair of 07 class shunters that became the final delivery from R&H in November 1962, bringing the Docks total to 14. As No 07013 it was also one of the last to leave the docks when withdrawn from service in July 1977. After refurbishment by Resco at Woolwich from May 1978 (where it was given their number L101) it was subsequently sold to Dow Chemicals at Kings Lynn in October that year. It was eventually taken into preservation at the South Yorkshire Railway Preservation Society in August 1994 before transfer to the Barrow Hill Roundhouse Railway Centre in June 1999. After moving to Peak Rail at Rowsley in November 2003 it has been cosmetically restored, but it is not in working order.

D2997 as 07013 at Rowsley in 2007. (Jack Perry Archive Collection)

BR Southampton Docks 0-6-0DE Ruston & Hornsby No 480699

Manufacturer:	Ruston & Hornsby Ltd
Built:	1962
Works number:	480699
Running numbers:	D2998 (BR)
At the docks:	1962 – 1973

One of the last arrivals to take its place at Southampton Docks, D2998 took up duty there in November 1962, but its time in the port was the shortest of all the 07s there because early withdrawal came in May 1973. After a spell of employment at BREL's Eastleigh Works it was scrapped in August 1976, never having received its TOPS number of 07014.

D2998 at Eastleigh on 10th March 1974. (Jack Perry)

Docks Engineer's Department 1928 – 1977

With the huge expansion of the docks already underway in 1928, the Engineers Department at Southampton Docks took on their own locomotives for use in lesser building projects and sundry works. The first such engine was *The Master General,* which arrived from the Mersey Docks & Harbour Board in April of that year. Built by Andrew Barclay as No 1188 in 1911 it was used initially during the construction of three 7 ft diameter culverts that would carry water from outlets along the foreshore of the West Bay to the new quayside at berth 101 where a pumping station was built. The culverts also carried cooling water to the town Power Station, which was situated near Southampton West (now Central) Station. (See the chapter on Southampton Power Station for details of their locomotives.)

During the construction of the New (Western) Docks, a new yard was laid out for the Engineers Department immediately to the west of the carriage shed, and from the mid 1930s their locos were housed there in the open. In 1935 *The Master General* was joined by a strange and much less conventional companion. A Motor Rail Simplex diesel mechanical engine (No 5355/1932) was purchased from T.W. Ward's Leeds Depot by the Southern Railway Docks Department. Although the diminutive loco was designed for 2 ft gauge rails it was rebuilt for operating on the standard gauge of the docks system and used for transporting permanent way tools and materials, which were towed on a trolley.

"The Master General" engaged in culvert laying works near the Pirelli factory on 4th June 1929.
(Associated British Ports)

A FURTHER LOOK AT SOUTHAMPTON'S QUAYSIDE RAILWAYS

Apart from a short replacement by an on-loan McAlpine loco (Hudswell Clarke No 1538/1924) in June 1939, *The Master General* toiled on unaided until being disposed of after the Second World War. Its place was taken by a Fowler 0-4-0 diesel mechanical shunter No 22934 built in 1941 for use in an ordnance factory in County Durham. The loco was numbered 400S when taken into Southern Railway departmental stock and arrived at the Western Docks Engineer's Yard in 1946. Here it was gainfully employed until being sold off in 1957, leaving just the adapted Simplex for the more menial tasks until that became obsolete in 1970 and its duties were taken over by a Wickham railcar (No 7974/1958), which lasted until about 1974 when it moved to Purley. The Simplex was finally disposed of in 1977 when the derelict works yard was demolished. From that time, materials were handled by BR locomotives based in the docks.

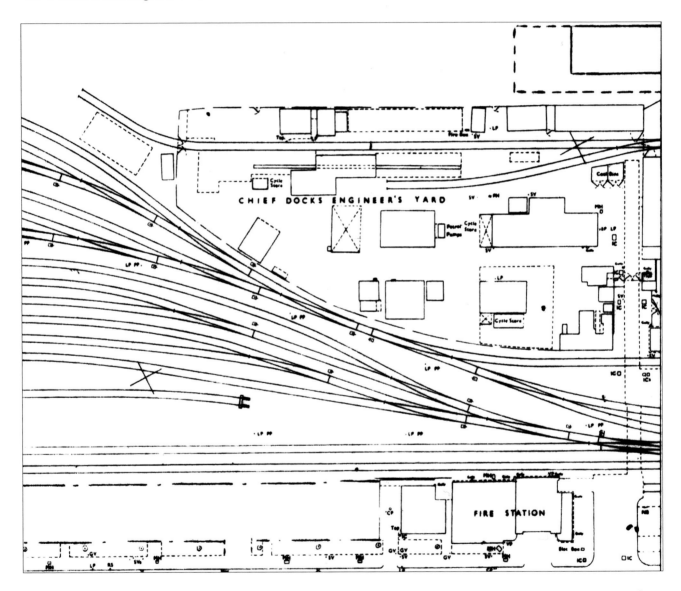

The Engineer's Yard as laid out in the New (Western) Docks in the 1930s. The various departmental locos were stored in the open sidings.

"The Master General" at work in the docks in Southern Railway days. (Jeff Pain Collection)

Southampton Docks Engineer's Department loco No 400S – Fowler No 22934 stands beside a pile of permanent way chairs in the New Docks on 5th January 1948. (John A. Bailey/Bert Moody Collection)

"The Master General" in storage at Eastleigh Works on 29ᵗʰ April 1948. (John A. Bailey/Bert Moody Collection)

A few rusting rails and dilapidated buildings signal the demise of the Engineer's works yard on 18ᵗʰ July 1975. Demolition came soon afterwards. (Author)

Docks Engineer's Department 0-4-0DM Fowler No 22934

Manufacturer:	John Fowler & Co Ltd, Leeds
Built:	1941
Works number:	22934
Running numbers:	ROF 9 No 1 (WD), 400S (SR), DS400 (BR), TWW No 3434
Driving wheels:	3ft 3in
Wheelbase:	6ft 3in
Engine:	150hp Fowler 4C
Weight:	29ton 0cwt
At the docks:	1946 – 1957

This Fowler loco was completed in January 1941 and saw military service at the Royal Ordnance Factory in Aycliffe, County Durham. After the hostilities of WWII ceased it was sold in November 1946 to the Southern Railway who employed it in their Western Docks Engineer's Department yard after the departure of 0-4-0ST *The Master General.* Its duties were mainly involved on civil engineering works projects and moving construction materials around the docks. Under British Railways it was renumbered DS400, but by September 1957 it had been disposed of to Thos. W. Ward at Grays, Essex where it carried the plant number TWW No 3434. During its time with Wards it was based at their Silvertown premises during 1959 – 1960 and was on loan to S. Williams at Dagenham Dock in May 1960, returning to TWW's Grays depot in September that year. Almost immediately it was sold to Eagre Construction of Scunthorpe who employed it in track lifting contracts, but nothing further is recorded.

New recruit Fowler 400S finds peacetime service with the Docks Engineer's Department, seen here at the Western Docks on 29th November 1950. (Author's Collection)

Docks Engineer's Department 4wPM Motor Rail No 5355

Manufacturer:	Motor Rail Ltd, Simplex Works, Bedford.
Built:	1932
Works number:	5355
Engine:	20/35 hp Dorman 4MRX
Weight:	2ton 10cwt
Gauge:	2ft 0in
At the docks:	1935 – 1977

This loco was turned out by the makers on 4th January 1933 and, along with three others (numbers 5365, 5379 and 5383) was delivered to contractor Samuel Johnson & Son (Mirfield) Ltd who employed it in the construction of Fly Flatts Reservoir at Wainstalls, Halifax. It was also used by another contractor at a Coventry sewage works before being purchased by T.W. Ward at their Albion Depot in Leeds in May 1935. Ward's then resold the loco to the Southern Railway Docks Department at Southampton in August that year, where it was based at the Engineer's yard in the New (Western) Docks and converted to standard gauge for use around the docks system. There it usually hauled a trolley laden with tools and materials used in minor works and repairs to the docks permanent way.

There had previously been some thought that the loco had come to the Docks Engineers by way of the John Mowlem contract for the King George V Graving Dock but there is no record to substantiate this.

In 1977 the old Engineer's yard had become derelict and new premises were acquired. By June that year, the obsolete loco was sold to Mr T.W. Smith at his riverside premises in Bitterne Park, Southampton, where it remained until the property was vacated in 2004. The loco was subsequently purchased by Messrs C. Billinghurst and P. Gray who removed it from site in July 2005, when the boatyard was cleared, and work is in progress to restore the engine to its original narrow gauge design, after which it will run on the Twyford Waterworks Railway, near Winchester.

The docks Simplex loco (Motor Rail No 5355/1932) was in a sorry state at the Engineer's yard when it was photographed there on 24th September 1972. (Keith Gunner)

Docks Engineer's Department 4wPM Wickham No 7974

Manufacturer:	D. Wickham & Co Ltd, Ware, Herts.
Built:	1958
Works number:	7974
Running numbers:	DB 965143
Driving wheels:	1ft 4in
Wheelbase:	3ft 2in
Engine:	10hp Ford
Weight:	20ton 0cwt
At the docks:	1970 – 1974

This example of the Wickham rail vehicle was of type 27A being a Mk III gang trolley supplied new to the Southern Region of BR at Warminster, Wilts in January 1958. By April 1963 it was recorded at Eastleigh and its next sighting was when on loan to the Docks Engineer's Department at Southampton's Western Docks. Capable of carrying up to 10 personnel, the trolley transported permanent way staff around the docks estate, while having an even smaller flat topped wagon in tow with tools and materials for minor jobs. It seems possible that this vehicle took over from the (by now) obsolete converted Motor Rail loco some time in 1970 and was certainly in evidence there in September of that year. By the mid 1970s the semi-derelict engineer's yard was all but closed and the Wickham had moved on to Purley. Then, in 1976-77, it was converted to a 2-ton trailer at Stewarts Lane before ending its days at Redhill, where it was scrapped in April 1990.

Wickham Rail Trolley No 7974 on docks duty for the Engineer's Department is pictured alongside the Western Docks Carriage Shed with one of the more conventional Ruston loco fleet in the background. (Jeff Pain)

This photograph taken in 1908 shows several TJR locos working in the muddy hollow that was to become the Ocean Dock. (Author's Collection)

Docks Contractors 1886 – 1999

During the construction of the Empress Dock from 1886, and at each later stage in the growth of Southampton's Docks, a succession of contractors' locomotives was employed in the various works, often labouring away for years on end, creating mammoth earthworks and concrete structures for the various quays. Although this subject was comprehensively covered in the previous volume, additional information and photographs have since become available.

White Star Dock – Topham, Jones & Railton, 1908 – 1911

The contract for the White Star Dock (now Ocean Dock) was undertaken by the firm of Topham, Jones & Railton. The dock, covering some 15.5 acres, had 3,800ft of new quays (berths 43 to 47) and offered the world's largest vessels a minimum 40ft of water at low tide. During its construction, between 1908 and 1911, TJR employed 12 standard gauge locos for the main work and, in addition, a couple of metre gauge engines in their block making plant. These were Bagnall inverted saddle tanks (IST) whereby the tank was positioned under the smokebox, rather than over the boiler, one thought being to provide greater stability on a small narrow engine. Nos 1447 and 1449 were built in 1895.

The block yard was set up between what is now 46 berth and the Trafalgar Drydock with concrete mixers at its southern end. These poured their contents into small tip wagons which ran on an elevated railway over the block moulds into which the material was discharged. The completed blocks were placed on wagons and hauled away to the quay wall construction by the locos. Concrete was also transported to other parts of the site by the narrow gauge lines.

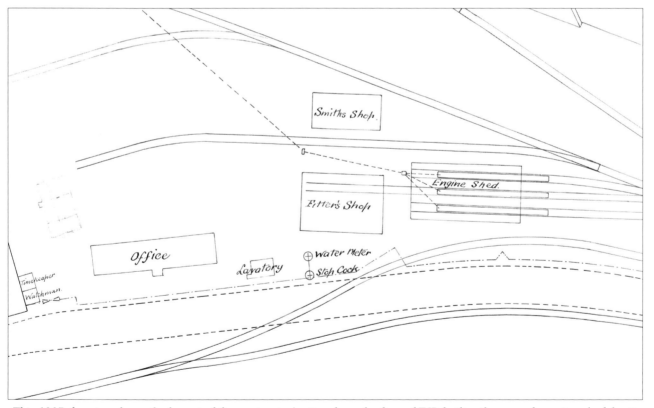

This 1907 drawing shows the layout of the contractor's site where the firm of TJR built a three-road running shed for its engines on the eastern side of the works. The area was afterwards developed as berths 43/4, from where the Titanic set sail in 1912. (Author's Collection)

Topham Contract Locomotive 0-4-0IST Bagnall No 1447

Manufacturer:	W.G. Bagnall Ltd, Castle Engine Works, Stafford.
Built:	1895
Works number:	1447
Running numbers:	21
Cylinders:	8in x 12in
Driving wheels:	2ft 0.5in
Wheelbase:	3ft 6in
Gauge:	Metre
At the docks:	1908 – 1910

No 1447 was delivered new to the Admiralty at Gibraltar in April 1895. By 1899 it had passed into the hands of Topham, Jones & Railton and was employed there on their dockyard contract, remaining until at least 1905. It was next recorded at Southampton Docks during Topham's building of the White Star (now Ocean) Dock, which was commenced in 1908. There it was engaged in the plant for making concrete blocks. After its stint at the docks, the loco is thought to have been put up for sale in June 1910 at the contractor's Cardiff Depot and nothing further is known.

Topham Contract Locomotive 0-4-0IST Bagnall No 1449

Manufacturer:	W.G. Bagnall Ltd, Castle Engine Works, Stafford.
Built:	1895
Works number:	1449
Running numbers:	33
Cylinders:	8in x 12in
Driving wheels:	2ft 0.5in
Wheelbase:	3ft 6in
Gauge:	Metre
At the docks:	1908 – 1911

Like its sister (No 1447) No 1449 was delivered new to the Admiralty at Gibraltar in May 1895 and became part of the Topham, Jones & Railton's dockyard contract fleet there by 1899. With the works completed in 1906 its return to Britain saw work at another TJR contract, this time at King's Dock, Swansea, and although that project lasted until 1909, it was subsequently engaged at Southampton during the building of the White Star (Ocean) Dock from 1908. Having worked with No 1447 in the block yard, the dock was completed in 1911, after which little else is known of its movements but spares for this loco were delivered to TJR's Swansea depot in November 1918 and it is assumed the engine saw further service after that date.

A rare photo of TJR's "Wymondley" (MW 1331/1897), which was one of the locos used in the building of the White Star Dock. This was taken in 1907 at the Hall Green shed of previous owners C.J. Wills during the construction of the Birmingham and North Warwickshire line. (Industrial Railway Society)

New Docks – Sir Robert McAlpine, 1927 – 1934

The largest of all the pre-WWII dock projects was the building of the New (Western) Docks by Sir Robert McAlpine and Sons from 1927 to 1934 (in conjunction with the King George Graving Dock undertaken by John Mowlem and Edmund Nuttall). During this time, McAlpine's engaged 19 standard gauge locos in building the new quays (berths 101 to 109), the quays being 7,000 ft in length. They also used narrow gauge systems for minor works, but details of these and their locomotives are somewhat scarce. However, two Motor Rail Simplex locomotives, numbers 4578 and 4580 are known to have been engaged during the works. Both were delivered new in 1930 and in all probability were used on many other McAlpine works after they left Southampton.

As the New (Western) Docks begin to take shape, debris is scattered across the site of what will become Mayflower Park. Rail mounted cranes and a McAlpine loco stand on the temporary rail tracks on 12th April 1931. The newly completed building on the right is the Stormwater Pumping Station at berth 101. (Tony Chilcott Collection)

McAlpine No 26 (Hudswell Clarke No 888/1909) stands alongside the newly built quays at 101 berth on 25th September 1932. (H.F. Wheeller)

Another line up of McAlpine locos at 101 berth features No 30 (Hudswell Clarke No 1011 /1912) on 25th September 1932. (H.F. Wheeller)

McAlpine No 46 (Hudswell Clarke No 1539/1924) seeks shelter inside one of the newly constructed cargo sheds on 25th September 1932. (H.F. Wheeller)

McAlpine Contract Locomotive 4wPM Motor Rail No 4578

Manufacturer:	Motor Rail Ltd, Simplex Works, Bedford.
Built:	1930
Works number:	4578
Engine:	20 hp Dorman 2JO
Weight:	2ton 10cwt
Gauge:	2ft 0in
At the docks:	1930

The first of two Simplex locos delivered new to McAlpine in May 1930 during their contract for building Southampton's New (Western) Docks. After a short spell there McAlpines transferred this loco to another of their construction sites at Dunston Power Station, Northumberland in November that year, but nothing further is recorded.

McAlpine Contract Locomotive 4wPM Motor Rail No 4580

Manufacturer:	Motor Rail Ltd, Simplex Works, Bedford.
Built:	1930
Works number:	4580
Engine:	20 hp Dorman 2JO
Weight:	2ton 10cwt
Gauge:	2ft 0in
At the docks:	1930

This standard design 20hp Simplex loco was the second delivered new to Sir Robert McAlpine at Southampton during their contract for building the New (Western) Docks. Like its sister (No 4578), it arrived at the Town Quay sidings in May 1930 and was employed in the construction works. It may then have accompanied No 4578 to the Dunston Power Station contract in November that year and, being still fairly new, was probably used on other projects by McAlpine afterwards.

King George V Drydock – John Mowlem, 1931 – 1935

The firm of John Mowlem (together with co-contractor Edmund Nuttall) was engaged to construct what was then the largest drydock in the world. The King George V Graving Dock was built between 1931 and 1935 and during that time Mowlem's had an on-site running shed that was home to 18 locomotives. The Drydock was officially opened by King George V on 26th July 1933,

although auxiliary works continued for another couple of years. This was a monumental project whereby over 1,250,000 cubic yards of material were excavated. The floor of the dock is 25 feet thick and the entire structure (1200ft long, 165ft wide and 60ft deep) contains some 456,000 cubic yards of concrete.

Mowlem's Hawthorn Leslie No 3760/1932 "Beaulieu" at work on the Drydock site. (Author's Collection)

During the drydock construction a temporary jetty was built for the transport of spoil by barges. Here, a Mowlem locomotive discharges tipper wagons on 15th October 1931. (Associated British Ports)

A muck-spattered "Penn" (MW No 1539/1902) awaits a turn of duty near the drydock shed. This veteran had been rebuilt prior to purchase by Mowlem at the start of the contract. (H.F. Wheeller)

HE No 1688/1931 "Southern" with running mates at the Mowlem shed taken on 25th September 1932.
(H.F. Wheeller)

Another of the Mowlem fleet "Nuttall" (HE No 1685/1931) is pictured at the same location. (Author's Collection)

Andrew Barclay No 1993/1932 "Shirley" takes on fuel and water for another long shift.   (H.F. Wheeller)

One of Mowlem's larger locos was "Blythe" (Avonside No 1894/1922) seen here in later years at the National Coal Board's Rossington Colliery on 23ʳᵈ May 1964. (A. Swain)

Also on the move after its Southampton duties was HE No 1690/1931 "Cunarder", which first went to co-contractor Edmund Nuttall in 1935 before ending its working days at the APCM's Harbury Works where it is pictured above. (Hugh Davies)

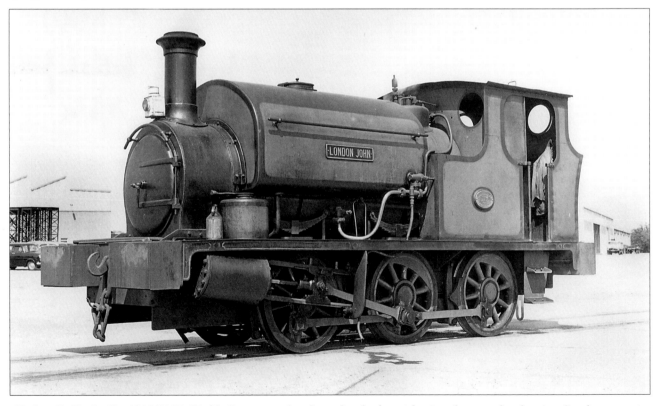

Hudswell Clarke No 1593/1927 "Bobby" was another loco that had an identity change after leaving Southampton in 1935, receiving the name "London John" when transferred to another Mowlem contract at Chingford Reservoir. It is shown here at Mowlem's Welham Green Depot on 24th June 1961. (Author's Collection)

Ford Vehicle Sidings – Trackwork, 1999

The most recent contractor's engine to be employed at the docks was during the works to construct sidings at the Ford Vehicle Handling Centre at the rear of 108 berth in the Western Docks, this being carried out by Trackwork Ltd of Doncaster. The tracks run from the main docks railway entrance at No 12 gate and handle imported vehicles, which are then distributed by road to UK locations. Ruston & Hornsby 4wDM No 412572 was employed on the site between January and April 1999 before moving on to other locations.

Trackwork Contract Loco 4wDM Ruston No 512572

Manufacturer:	Ruston & Hornsby Ltd, Lincoln
Built:	1965
Works number:	512572
Engine:	88hp Ruston 4VPO
Driving wheels:	3ft 0in
Wheelbase:	5ft 10in
Weight:	17ton 0cwt
At the docks:	1999

This Ruston loco was one of a pair employed on various contracts by the firm of Trackwork Ltd of Long Sandall, Doncaster. Having arrived at Southampton in January 1999 it was engaged in the construction of sidings for the Ford Vehicle Centre in the Western Docks, remaining at work there until April when it left the site for another contract. It is now in preservation and operational on the Epping & Ongar Railway where it has been reunited with its former running mate.

Ruston No 512572 at work on the new sidings at Southampton Docks in 1999. (Paul Gosling)

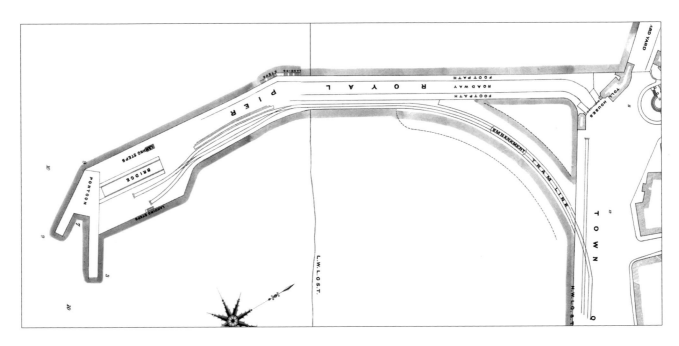

The original Pier Station consisted of just one open platform as shown in the 1888 map above. The pier itself was enlarged and extended in 1892 as was the station in the 1918 drawing below.

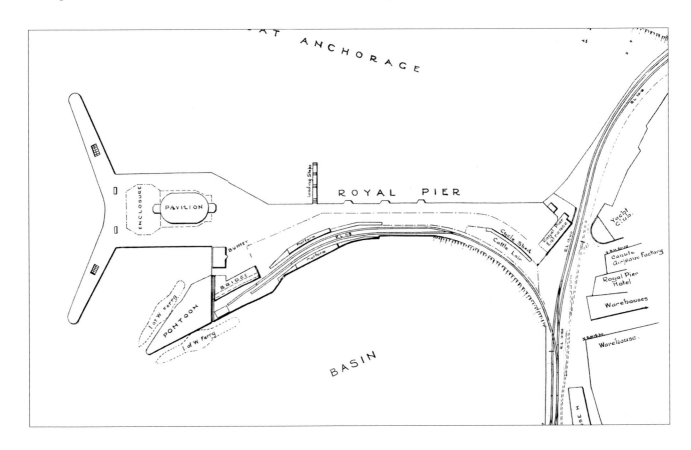

Town Quay and Royal Pier 1847 – 1970

Despite their prime location on Southampton's waterfront, the Town Quay and Royal Pier were always administered separately from the Docks, firstly by the Harbour Commissioners and latterly by the Harbour Board, which was finally amalgamated with the Docks in 1968.

A tramway from Southampton Town Station (later Terminus) to the Town Quay had been laid down in 1847 and extended to the Royal Pier in 1871. Both lines were operated by the LSWR, with traffic being initially horse drawn until the Pier service had its own dedicated engines from 1876. These were small 0-4-0ST locos built by Alexander Shanks and Son of Arbroath, and carried the names *Southampton, Cowes,* and *Ritzbuttel,* which over the ensuing years also became engaged in Town Quay shunting until other small tank engines took over. While the Royal Pier service officially ceased in 1914, the Town Quay traffic survived into BR years until closure in 1970.

"Southampton" was the first of the Shanks locos to operate the pier service and is pictured at the station in the late 1800s. (HMRS Collection)

*Shanks 0-4-0ST No 468/1873 "Ritzebuttel" with a train at the rebuilt Pier Station circa 1900.
(Bert Moody Collection)*

THE ROYAL PIER, SOUTHAMPTON

The ailing Royal Pier passenger service had officially ceased at the outbreak of WWI and the line was already in advanced decay by the time a steamer had hit the pier causing damage to both the structure and the track upon it. This early 1920s photograph shows the damaged area removed, while the track beyond it has been lifted and only the eastern station canopy survives. (Author's Collection)

Railway company wagons line waterfront between the Town Quay and Royal Pier in February 1927. In the background, beyond the Pier can be seen the remains of the Military train ferry jetty but all this was soon to change. (Tony Chilcott Collection)

After the Southern Railway's decision to extend the docks across the West Bay, preliminary works in 1927 included widening of the roadways and rail tracks along the Town Quay frontage and the area between the Quay and Pier was reclaimed to allow this. The wider thoroughfare was then able to carry contractor's trains to another reclamation site on the west side of the pier. That area was for the reception of materials for the docks construction and eventually became Mayflower Park. The widening of road and rail along the waterfront also saw the removal of the original Royal Pier entrance which was replaced by the building that now stands in front of the currently derelict pier.

Past and present stand together in November 1929 as the old Royal Pier entrance (on the right) faces demolition. The railway will be realigned in front of the newly completed building behind it. (Tony Chilcott Collection)

Long after the demise of the Royal Pier Railway, the Town Quay line continued to flourish with regular trains being assembled for daily collection. Over the years, much of the shunting was carried out by the diminutive locos of the C14 class, which were ideally suited to the tight curves on the quay itself. However, when the class became extinct, the replacement diesels were unable to negotiate certain areas, and in such circumstances a road bumper was employed to manoeuvre wagons for collection. The diesels were usually of the 0-6-0DM Drewry type sent along from the Terminus yard, or directly from Eastleigh, with numbers D2289 and D2291 being amongst the most regular callers until traffic ceased in 1970.

Opposite page, top: The congestion of road and rail traffic along the Town Quay and Royal Pier waterfront is clearly visible in this photograph from the early 1920s. (Tony Chilcott Collection)

Opposite page, bottom: March 1927 and work has begun on reclaiming the area between the Quay and Pier. The added frontage would eventually carry the connecting railway between the Old and New Docks and was later extended further to accommodate the present Red Funnel Ferry Terminal. (Tony Chilcott Collection)

C14 No 3741 in action on the Town Quay sidings on 24th March 1950. (John A. Bailey/Bert Moody Collection)

This 1943 vintage Fordson/Chaseside tractor is pictured on the Town Quay where it was employed in shunting duties after the C14 locos were scrapped. The wire strop was used to haul wagons along to more accessible areas where a diesel loco could take over. The tractor was purchased privately in 1974, following several years in storage after rail operations had ceased. It has now been fully restored and is once again operational. (Author's Collection)

Train Ferries 1917 – 1922 and 1943 – 1946

During the dark days of the two world wars, a number of train ferry terminals were constructed at Southampton. The first was constructed in 1917 to speed supplies to the military in France during the Great War. A line was constructed from the south side of Southampton West (now Central) Station and ran alongside Western Esplanade on a reclaimed strip of the West Bay foreshore until reaching a jetty built just to the west of the Royal Pier. The traffic was worked by two locomotives, one being a Kerr, Stuart 0-6-0T No 3067 built in 1917 and the other being an unidentified Peckett 0-4-0ST, both were operated by the military.

Although the tracks along Western Esplanade were lifted by the early 1920s, the jetty remained in place and

became a useful facility during the construction of the New (Western) Docks. It was first used to pump dredged material ashore during the initial reclamation works, which formed the land now occupied by Mayflower Park. Once this area was established it became the site for the contractor's concrete mixing plant.

Further rail-connected ferry landing stages were built during World War Two, one being just to the east of the Royal Pier and another to the west of the King George V Graving Dock. These were for shipping out goods, munitions and ambulance trains for the D-Day invasion, and latterly to return allied troops and prisoners of war to the UK.

US Army Transportation Corps diesel locos Nos 7926 and 8583 with rolling stock being loaded aboard a train ferry adjacent to King George V Drydock on 12th July 1944. The saddle tank loco on the extreme right is possibly RSH No 7110/1943. (Tony Chilcott Collection)

This photograph taken from an old press cutting shows the train ferry line from Southampton West station leading off to the right towards Western Esplanade circa 1918. (KRM Collection)

The former WWI train ferry jetty was utilised during reclamation works for the New Docks construction. Here, it supports a pipeline bringing dredged material ashore from the vessel "Riparian" in 1928. (Tony Chilcott collection)

The railhead alongside the Royal Pier saw German prisoners ferried to Britain during the latter stages of the war. This photograph was taken in March 1945. (Author's collection)

Southampton Power Station 1904 – 1964

In the days before nationalisation (and subsequent privatisation) most towns owned and managed their own utility supplies of gas, water and electricity. Parliamentary consent for a new Southampton power station was sought in 1903 and the plant became a reality in the following year. The site chosen was on the (then) foreshore of the West Bay, just east of Southampton West railway station.

The generating station was built on reclaimed land at the water's edge and a rail connection made to the main line midway between the West station and the town tunnel. A siding ran south across Western Shore Road (now Western Esplanade) to a system that ran though the works and on to a jetty.

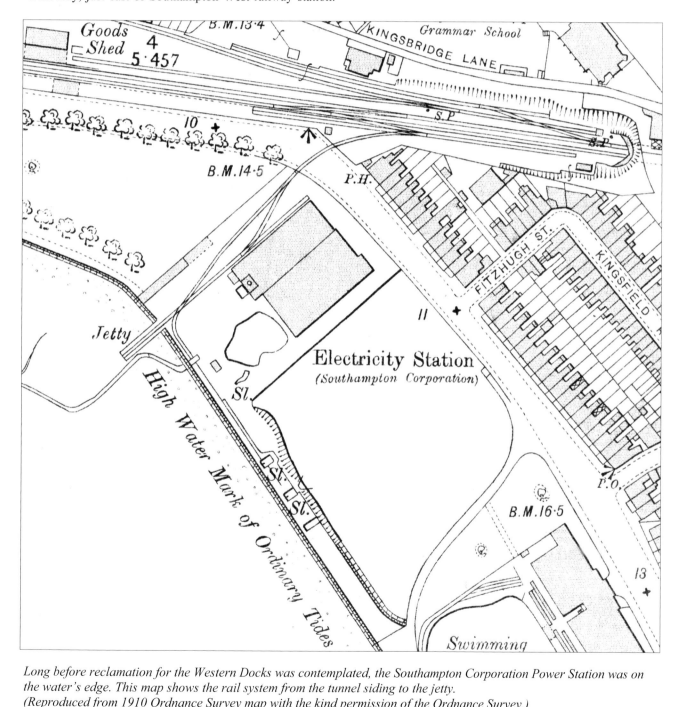

Long before reclamation for the Western Docks was contemplated, the Southampton Corporation Power Station was on the water's edge. This map shows the rail system from the tunnel siding to the jetty.
(Reproduced from 1910 Ordnance Survey map with the kind permission of the Ordnance Survey.)

A FURTHER LOOK AT SOUTHAMPTON'S QUAYSIDE RAILWAYS

Initially, coal was brought in from the siding by horse drawn wagons but plans were made for motorised traction in 1904. With all the coal available, it could be supposed that a steam locomotive would be the logical mode, but Southampton Corporation decided to make use of the technology already employed on its tram system. Overhead power lines were erected from the exchange siding, across the road, and around the works, with the first locomotive being built on site from a variety of spare parts from the Tramway Department.

The "new" locomotive commenced operation on the 16th December 1904 after the 550-volt system had been declared safe, although rail movements were restricted to a maximum of four miles per hour. The coal came mostly from the Chapel Wharves along the River Itchen and was carried in privately purchased wagons to the exchange siding where the 0-4-0 electric loco would collect and convey them into the works.

The amount of coal needed, and number of wagons used, grew steadily over the years and by 1930 the loco, known as Southampton Corporation Electricity Department No 1, was deemed unable to cope, so a new

locomotive was ordered from makers Baguley at Burton-upon-Trent, and No 2 (Works No 2048) was supplied in 1931. The new 4-wheel engine was certainly needed as, by the end of the decade, the number of wagons handled had risen to an average 50 a day during the winter months, deeming a third loco necessary.

No 3 came from makers Greenwood & Batley (No 1620) and arrived new in 1939. It was the last of the power station locos, and the trio worked together until Nationalisation of the industry, after which the ageing No 1 was taken out of service and scrapped in 1953. The remaining two saw out their days until the coal deliveries were switched to road transport and the pair was broken up on site by local firm Pollock & Brown in March 1960. The connection to the main line was eventually severed in April 1964 with the rails across the roadway being lifted some five months later.

With the coming of the national grid, and large regional power stations, such local generation plants became redundant and the works were finally dismantled in 1977 The site is now occupied by a retail unit in the shape of Toys R Us.

Southampton Power Station No 2 pictured on the exchange sidings in the 1930s with the town tunnel in the background. (Bert Moody collection)

Southampton Power Station from the air circa 1928 with the cooling pond in the foreground. The rail connection to the power station can clearly be seen crossing the roadway from the main line. To the north is Southampton West (now Central) railway station and at the bottom left is the old public baths with its outside pool. Down the left side of the picture works are in progress in laying down the 7 ft diameter stormwater culvert pipes prior to the infilling of the West Bay for the docks extension. (Southampton City Archive)

Southampton Power Station 0-4-0WE SCED No 1

Manufacturer:	Southampton Corporation Electricity Department
Built:	1904
Running numbers:	No 1
At Western Esplanade:	1904 – 1953

Soon after the opening of the power station, this locomotive was constructed by the Southampton Corporation from materials and oddments available from the town's tramway system at the very modest cost of £146.00. This unpretentious little engine bore the brunt of the works traffic until assistance was called for, and a second loco acquired, in 1931. It then continued to give excellent service for almost half a century until disposed of as scrap in 1953.

Southampton Power Station 4wWE Baguley No 2048

Manufacturer:	Baguley (Engineers) Ltd, Burton-upon-Trent. Staffordshire
Built:	1931
Works number:	2048
Running numbers:	No 2
Engine:	100hp
At Western Esplanade:	1931 – 1960

Southampton Power Station's second locomotive cost considerably more than its original engine when purchased new for £1139.00 in 1931 from makers Baguley Engineering. Its uninterrupted years of service ended when it was scrapped, along with the yard's other remaining loco (GB No 1620), by local firm Pollock Brown & Co in March 1960.

Southampton Power Station 4wWE Greenwood & Batley No 1620

Manufacturer:	Greenwood & Batley Ltd, Leeds
Built:	1939
Works number:	1620
Engine:	100hp
At Western Esplanade:	1939 – 1960

This was the power station's third and final loco, which was delivered new from the makers in 1939 at a cost of £1595.00. Along with the others, it worked through the wartime years and beyond until losing running mate No 1 in 1953, and meeting its own end in March 1960 when scrapped on site with Baguley No 2048 by local firm Pollock Brown & Co.

Southampton Power Station No 1 was an 0-4-0 overhead electric loco built in 1904 by Southampton Corporation and is pictured at work on 3ʳᵈ August 1950. (John A. Bailey/Bert Moody Collection)

Southampton Power Station's second loco was Baguley No 2048 of 1931 vintage photographed on site on 3ʳᵈ August 1950. (John A. Bailey/Bert Moody Collection)

Greenwood & Batley No 1620, built in 1939, was the power station's last acquisition and was photographed in action on 3ʳᵈ August 1950. (John A. Bailey/Bert Moody Collection)

Left: The rail crossing at Western Esplanade to the Power Station photographed in 1964, shortly before the rails were lifted. The Civic Centre clock tower can be seen in the background.
(Jeff Pain)

Below: Southampton Power Station viewed from the Southern Railway Central Station in 1938. Note the new Art deco façade of the entrance to the down platforms.
(Eric Thompson Collection – Bitterne Local History Society)

CHAPTER 7

Millbrook Foundry 1836 – 1845

By 1836, the firm of Summers, Groves and Day had established an engineering business in an ironworks situated at the bottom of what is now Foundry Lane. They manufactured engines and boilers before venturing into shipbuilding, but there were difficulties in launching vessels in having to haul them across Millbrook Road to the nearby Mill Place Quay on the shore of the West Bay (which was later reclaimed for the building of the New Docks). By 1840 they had established a new shipyard at Northam on a site that became Northam Ironworks (see Chapter 19), but the Foundry Road works were retained for the construction of locomotives, firstly for road and then for the railway.

There are no precise records of how many railway engines they built there, but at least two were constructed for the London and Southampton Railway (later the LSWR) in 1839. The first was *Fly* – a four wheeled 16hp loco, which ran trials on the railway in May that year and

was purchased by the L&SR in June. It was originally named *Garnett* after one of the major shareholders but that was soon changed. The second was a more powerful engine named *Southampton,* which came into railway ownership the following August, and although these may be considered "main line" engines, which is contrary to the theme of this book, their uniqueness in local railway history warrants inclusion. Both worked on the Southampton to Winchester section, as the continuation of the main line to London was not complete until May the following year.

The Millbrook Works continued to turn out engines, mainly for marine purposes, until at least 1845 when, following expansion at the Northam Yard it is presumed the manufacturing plant moved there. It would appear that their attempts at locomotive building were largely unsuccessful, and the enterprise was abandoned around the time of the move to Northam.

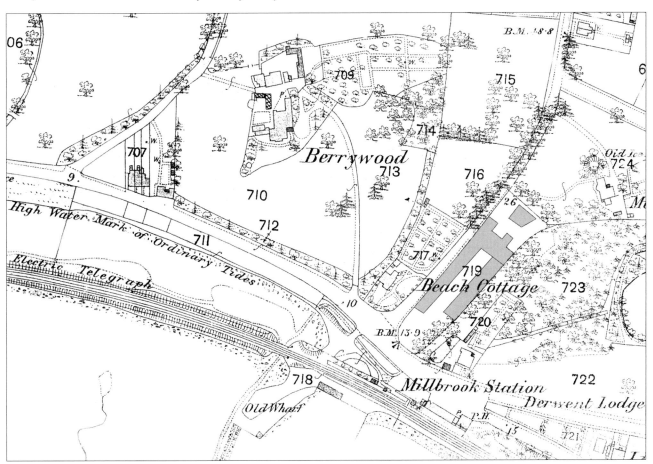

The foundry had long since disappeared by the time this 1867 map displayed the railway and Millbrook station on the shore of the West Bay, but its outline has been superimposed in the area of Beach Cottage to show its position at the bottom of Foundry Lane. Mill House Quay was still in evidence as the Old Wharf.
(Reproduced from 1867 Ordnance Survey map with the kind permission of the Ordnance Survey.)

L&SR 2-2-0 Summers

Name:	*(Garnett) Fly*
Manufacturer:	Summers, Groves & Day, Millbrook Foundry, Southampton
Built:	1839
Running numbers:	40
Cylinders:	12in x 18in
Driving wheels:	5ft 6in
Weight:	13ton 0cwt
At Millbrook:	1839

Originally named *Garnett,* after one of the railway company shareholders, *Fly* was Summers first recorded locomotive built for the embryonic London & Southampton Railway, who had placed an order with them as early as August 1837. It appeared for trials in May 1839 and was purchased by the railway a month later at a cost of £1110.00.

Having worked the Southampton to Winchester section until the completed main line was opened in May 1840, the loco was found unable to handle the longer distances and required speed so was soon relegated to lesser tasks. Having been allocated the number 40, it sustained damage in a landslip at Fareham, and was returned to Millbrook for repairs in January 1842, but nothing more was heard of it until May 1843 when it was engaged in light shunting duties in the London area. Its failure seemed complete when relegated to the lowly status of pumping engine at Nine Elms in February 1846 before being taken out of service in October 1849. Its end came when it was finally broken up there in February 1851.

L&SR 2-2-2 Summers

Name:	*Southampton*
Manufacturer:	Summers, Groves & Day, Millbrook Foundry, Southampton
Built:	1839
Works number:	1846 (Fairburn)
Running numbers:	16 and 176
Cylinders:	13in x 18in (15in x 20in)
At Millbrook:	1839

Summers' second recorded loco for the L&SR was delivered in August 1839 and was only marginally more successful than their earlier engine *Fly.* At a cost of £1338.00 it too began life on the Southampton to Winchester section of the main line and, although larger and more powerful, *Southampton* soon proved troublesome by needing constant repairs once the completed main line to London was opened up in May 1840. By January 1841 its role had been reduced to that of providing hot water for the washing plant at Nine Elms, but it was reprieved when sent to Fairburn & Son for a rebuild which was completed in August 1844.

When re-launched as the railway's No 16 that December, it was given a new lease of life on rural services until once again relegated to the role of stationary boiler at Ringwood. Disposal had been considered by 1852 but a shortage of locos meant a second reprieve in 1853 and yet another rebuild took place under engineer Joseph Beattie in the middle of 1859.

Now renumbered 176 *Southampton* re-entered service and worked between Brockenhurst and Lymington, but by May 1862 it was back at Nine Elms for overhaul. In early 1863 it was dispatched to Northam Shed for further employment at Stokes Bay and Lymington. These duties lasted until April 1868 and by July that year it was working the Fareham to Gosport trains when cylinder problems forced yet another return to Nine Elms. There, it languished until being withdrawn in October 1869 and was eventually scrapped in the following January.

CHAPTER 8

Eling Tramway 1851 – 1993

Having been laid down and connected to the Southampton & Dorchester Railway in 1851, the tramway at Eling Wharf initially became an important landing place for timber products and, later, from 1920 became the main staging post for materials ferried down Southampton Water to Ashlett Creek during the construction of Fawley Refinery (see Chapter 13). In the ensuing years, several locomotives worked the line, which fed a number of industrial premises until its closure in 1993.

From 1923, the firm of Burt Boulton & Haywood, along with the adjacent South Western Tar Distilleries, employed a trio of steam locomotives until 1966, when the first (and only) privately owned diesel locomotive worked the system before traffic movements were carried out by BR locos from 1973.

The small Ruston diesel arrived, initially on hire, in May 1966 marking the demise of the line's last steam loco *Benton II* which was subsequently disposed of two months later. The small amount of rail traffic on the BB&H and SWTD sidings was easily handled by the Ruston, while rail mounted steam cranes continued to work the wharf, but from 1973 newer, heavier industries at Eling relied on BR main line engines to handle their freight, and the diminutive loco was disposed of in 1975 when the few remaining rail operations at the Tar Distilleries ceased.

A steam crane simmers on the quayside in a peaceful scene at Eling Wharf in 1952. (Author's Collection)

One of the tramway's first locomotives was 0-4-0ST "Benton" (Black Hawthorn No 1099 built 1896) which arrived from Woolston Rolling Mills in 1923 and is pictured at Eling Wharf on 15th May 1948. (John A. Bailey/Bert Moody Collection)

The oldest loco to work at Eling Wharf was an 1877 vintage Manning Wardle 0-4-0ST No 653 "Cameronian" also photographed on 15th May 1948. (John A. Bailey/Bert Moody Collection)

Eling Tramway 4wDM Ruston & Hornsby No 218044

Manufacturer:	Ruston & Hornsby Ltd, Lincoln
Built:	1942
Works number:	218044
Engine:	48hp Ruston 4VRO
Driving wheels:	2ft 6in
Wheelbase:	5ft 2in
Weight:	6ton 0cwt
At Eling:	1966 – 1975

Eling Wharf's solitary diesel shunter was supplied new in November 1942 to Dennis Bros Ltd at their Woodbridge Works in Guildford, where it carried the name *William* until 1962. It was then sold to Fred Watkins (Engineering) Ltd, a company that bought, sold and overhauled locos, and also operated a quarry plant at Coleford in Gloucester. It remained with Watkins until hired out to Burt Boulton and Haywood in May 1966 where it was subsequently purchased and worked until scrapped in July 1975.

Diesel days at Eling Wharf as Ruston No 218044 handles a Tar Distillery train in 1966. (Roger Holmes)

Above: Steam days at Eling Wharf are drawing to a close as the tramway's last 0-4-0ST, Andrew Barclay No 1290 "Benton II" built in 1912, works a train on the Tar Distillery lines. (Roger Holmes)

Left: A sad scene looking south from the Totton High Street level crossing towards the Burt Boulton & Haywood sidings on 22nd April 1993, with tracks removed after the tramway closure. (Dave Purvis)

Marchwood Power Station 1955 – 1963

To meet the energy demands of the growing population along the western side of Southampton water, the Central Electricity Authority built a power station at Marchwood located on the waterside just to the north of the Military port. Initial works began in 1953 and access by rail for materials was gained in 1955 via a link to the War Department rails, themselves being connected to the Totton to Fawley branch line. From that time, two locomotives were employed during the power station's construction. The first was a Robert Stephenson & Hawthorn 0-4-0ST No 7540, built in 1949, which arrived from Tilbury Power Station in 1955. The second was a Motor Rail four wheel diesel mechanical engine No 3966 of 1939 vintage.

After works were completed, the power station opened in 1957 and the RSH loco moved on to St John's Wood Power Station in London, while the Motor Rail loco remained on site seeing only sporadic use until moving to Earley Power Station at Reading in 1960. The disused track was finally lifted in 1963.

A larger generating station was built at Fawley in 1964-5 and the facility at Marchwood was closed and demolished in the early 1990s, the site being converted into an industrial park which was partly taken over by an incinerator. However, increasing demand for power has now led to the planned rebuilding of a new £400m gas fired plant on part of the original site, and this is due to come on line in 2009.

Marchwood Power Station pictured in 1960. Having been completed in 1955 it was demolished some four decades later, but a new generating station is due to replace it in the near future. (Southampton City Archive)

Marchwood Power Station 0-6-0ST Robert Stephenson & Hawthorn No 7540

Manufacturer:	Robert Stephenson & Hawthorn Ltd, Newcastle on Tyne
Built:	1949
Works number:	7540
Running number:	No 1 (No 3)
Cylinders:	14in x 22in
Driving wheels:	3ft 6in
Wheelbase:	5ft 6in
At Marchwood:	1955 – 1957

RSH No 7540 was built in May 1949 and supplied new to the British Electricity Authority at Grove Road Generating Station, St Johns Wood. By 1951, under the Central Electricity Authority, it had been transferred to Brunswick Wharf power station at Poplar. Two years later it had moved on to Tilbury, Essex from whence its onward journey took it to Marchwood by 1955. After construction of the Marchwood Power Station was completed, the loco returned to St Johns Wood in October 1957 where it was renumbered No 3 and worked there until eventually sent for scrap in 1964.

RSH No 7540 returned to St Johns Wood Generating Station and was photographed there in 1961.
(Frank Jones Collection/IRS)

Marchwood Power Station 4wDM Motor Rail No 3966

Manufacturer:	Motor Rail Ltd, Simplex Works, Bedford
Built:	1939
Works number:	3966 (previously 1943 & 2178)
Running numbers:	(3)
Engine:	40hp Dorman 4JO
Weight:	8ton 0cwt
At Marchwood:	1955 – 1961

This much rebuilt loco began life in December 1919 as Motor Rail No 1943 when supplied to the Central Cornwall China Clay Co Ltd at Pontsmill Sidings, St Blazey. After being badly damaged in a collision, it was rebuilt as No 2178 in 1933 and sold to Reads Ltd at Aintree in Liverpool. In November 1938 it again returned to Motor Rail for another rebuild, this time emerging as No 3966 in 1939 when it went to Vickers Armstrong at Blackpool in April that year. A month later it was with Petrol Loco Hirers (a subsidiary of Motor Rail) between May and August 1939 until sold on to Richard Leggott Chalk Quarries Ltd at South Ferriby, Lincolnshire. By 1955 it was in the hands of dealers George Drew of Oldham when purchased by the Electricity Board for use on the site at Marchwood where work was progressing on the new power station. It remained there until transfer to the Earley Power Station at Reading in September 1961. Running as their No 3 loco, its time there lasted until further travels took it to the East Yelland Power Station in Devon in January 1970. This became its final workplace until being sent for scrap to Messrs H. Slack at Exeter in January 1975.

CHAPTER 10

Marchwood Military Railway 1943 – Present Day

Before the Totton, Hythe and Fawley Light Railway was completed in 1925, the Admiralty had established a Magazine at Cracknore Hard, where workers were conveyed by boat across the River Test from Southampton's Royal Pier. A siding to the hard was built in 1939 and this developed into the military railway as the war years progressed.

The military port at Marchwood came into being in 1943 as preparations were being made for the invasion of Europe, and sections of the temporary Mulberry Harbour were assembled ready for transportation across the Channel. At its peak, the port railway had some 30 miles of track with three stations named "Mulberry Platform", "Park Gate" and "Model Room" for the conveyance of personnel around the complex which covers some 289 acres, and had facilities for 1500 troops. Known as the No 1 Port and Inland Water Transport Depot, it became home to the Royal Engineers 17 Port Regiment upon their formation in 1949.

From the early days until the 1960s, the motive power was supplied by locomotives from the Longmoor Military Railway and a succession of Austerity 0-6-0 saddle tanks were allocated there, usually two at a time. The regulars were *Spyck, Rennes, Constantine, Foligno,* and finally *Waggoner*, which was the last of the class to arrive somewhat later in 1973. During the 1950s, others were sighted at Marchwood but it is uncertain whether they were official allocations or just fleeting visits.

These locomotives were of a design (with the odd modification) built by seven different makers for the War Department, for which a total of 391 were turned out between 1943 and 1953. So successful was the Austerity saddle tank that a further 93 were completed by 1964 for civilian use and operation by the National Coal Board. Their main dimensions being:

Cylinders:	18in x 26in
Driving wheels:	4ft 3in
Wheelbase:	11ft 0in
Boiler pressure:	170psi
Weight:	48ton 2cwt
Coal capacity:	2ton 5 cwt
Water capacity:	1200gals

Longmoor had its own two-digit numbering system, but these never appeared on the locos themselves. The War Department fleet had been numbered in the 70,000s but in 1952, taking into account the number of losses, scrapping, and sales to private ownership, they adopted a new system in the 100s, with a further renumbering of army locos from 1968.

The locomotive allocations at Marchwood became more established as operations at Longmoor were wound down prior to its closure in 1969. The introduction of diesel power had come in 1960 but the late arrival of *Waggoner* was necessary to convey the local passenger stock around the camp due to the braking systems of the coaches. This it did until 1979, thus ending steam days at Marchwood. Since dieselisation (with the steam exception of *Waggoner*) the locos at Marchwood have been provided by a host of makers until more recent years when the military has favoured a standard Thomas Hill "Vanguard" 4-wheel design. The principle dimensions are:

Engine:	300hp Rolls-Royce C6FL
Driving wheels:	3ft 6in
Wheelbase:	9ft 0in
Weight:	35ton 0cwt

Over the years, many of the military locos have suffered identity transformations as names were exchanged and used repeatedly on different engines at different periods. The turnover of locomotives passing through the military port has been constant, with engines arriving and moving on to other locations on a regular basis and, as such, there has been an extraordinary number appearing at Marchwood as and when needs dictated.

In the past, the establishment has held periodic open days when members of the public were allowed to view and ride the rail system but, alas, such rare treats are no longer practical in today's political climate. Currently there are four diesel locomotives stationed at the military port, which is the only such installation in the UK and has latterly played a strategic role in moving arms and equipment to Iraq. Marchwood also acts as a staging post for locos in transit, and currently in store there, after returning from Romania in June 2005, are six Andrew Barclay locos numbers 663, 664, 665, 666, 667 and 668, all built in 1984.

A unique occasion as steam returned to Marchwood Military Port on 19th June 1993 for the naming of main line loco No 47213 as "Marchwood Military Port" (at rear). Standard class No 76017 "Sir Tristram" stands on No 2 jetty with the RFA vessel of the same name alongside. (Dave Purvis)

The scene at a Marchwood open day on 21st July 1979 with Ruston No 466623 on passenger duties alongside a visiting DMU that ran a special from Paddington, via Reading, Fareham and Bedenham. (Lee Snelling)

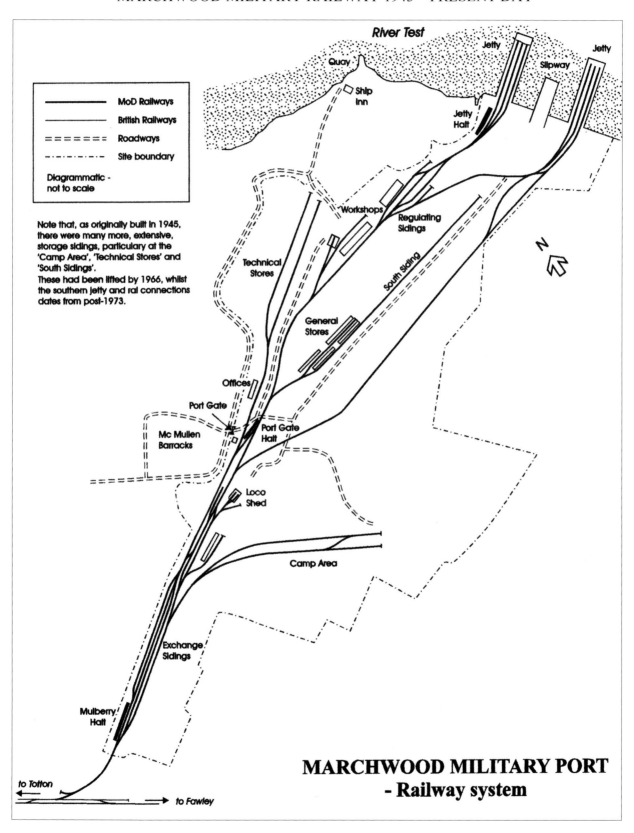

A diagrammatic representation of the Marchwood Military Railway system in the 1970s. (Map by Roger Hateley)

Marchwood Military Railway 0-6-0ST Hunslet No 2889

Name:	*Spyck*
Manufacturer:	Hunslet Engine Co Ltd, Hunslet, Leeds
Built:	1943
Works number:	2889
Running numbers:	32 (LMR), 75040 and 106
At Marchwood:	1948, 1955, and 1956 – 1960

No 2889 was one of the huge number of Austerity class 0-6-0 saddle tanks turned out by several makers during the Second World War. In this case it was the Hunslet Engine Co who delivered the loco to the War Department in 1943 and, as with others of the class, *Spyck* found itself on spells of duty at Marchwood. It was observed there in 1948 and by 1949 it was at the Longmoor Military Railway, from where it was loaned to the Port of London Authority between February and July 1954, afterwards finding its way back to Marchwood in May 1955. By October that year it was at the Hunslet Engine Co being rebuilt. It then returned to Marchwood in May 1956, remaining there until a final transfer to Longmoor in June 1960. In July 1963 it was sold for scrap to Woodham Brothers at Barry Docks where it was eventually broken up in March 1965.

Marchwood Military Railway 0-6-0ST Vulcan No 5280

Name:	*Manipur Road (Alexander)*
Manufacturer:	Vulcan Foundry Ltd, Newton-le-Willows
Built:	1945
Works number:	5280
Running numbers:	40 (LMR), 75290, and 186
At Marchwood:	1950 and 1953

This product of the Vulcan Foundry arrived new to Longmoor in June 1945 and originally carried the name *Alexander*. While based there it was reported as being sent for Marchwood duties in October 1950 and again reported there in June 1953 when it was replaced by RSH No 7139 *Rennes*. By February 1954 it had been sent for overhaul to the Hunslet Engine Co at Leeds before returning to Longmoor, and was eventually sold out of service to Hunslet in February 1961, who rebuilt it as HE No 3878 before selling it on to the National Coal Board's colliery at Mardy in Glamorganshire in October of that year. Its days at Mardy lasted until being scrapped on site by J.Cashmore Ltd in June 1971.

Marchwood Military Railway 0-6-0ST RSH No 7139

Name:	*Rennes*
Manufacturer:	Robert Stephenson & Hawthorns Ltd, Newcastle upon Tyne
Built:	1944
Works number:	7139 (3880 Hunslet rebuild in 1962)
Running numbers:	37 (LMR), 75189 and 152 (both WD), 8 (NCB)
At Marchwood:	1953 – 1956

This Robert Stephenson & Hawthorns version of the Austerity design was delivered to the War Department in 1944, and by 1949 was at Longmoor. After a trip to the makers for repairs in 1950 it was back at Longmoor in September of that year. By June 1953 it had arrived at Marchwood, its spell there lasting until May 1956 after which it returned to Longmoor where it remained until being sold as surplus to the Hunslet Engine Company in November 1960. Hunslet rebuilt the loco as their works No 3880, and in 1962 sold it to the National Coal Board at Mountain Ash, Glamorgan where it ended its working days in 1980 as No 8 before being taken into preservation at the Big Pit Mining Museum at Blaenavon.

Austerity Hunslet No 2889 "Spyck" on duty at Marchwood as No 75040 on 15th May 1948. (John A. Bailey/Bert Moody Collection)

Vulcan No 5280 "Manipur Road" pictured at Longmoor on 3rd September 1955. (R.K. Blencowe Collection)

RSH No 7139 "Rennes" as WD 152 at Marchwood on 25th April 1953. (M.H. Walshaw)

Marchwood Military Railway 0-6-0ST Robert Stephenson & Hawthorns No 7207

Name:	*Foligno*
Manufacturer:	Robert Stephenson & Hawthorns Ltd, Newcastle upon Tyne
Built:	1945
Works number:	7207
Running numbers:	38 (LMR), 75277 and 178
At Marchwood:	1954 – 1955

Foligno (originally intended to carry the name *Marlborough*) was the second RS&H version of the Austerity design to work at Marchwood. Having been supplied new to the War Department at Longmoor in March 1945, it became allocated to Marchwood in October 1954, its short spell there lasting only until April 1955 before returning to Longmoor. There it spent the remainder of its career, and in latter years was used for re-railing demonstrations until being sold as scrap to Woodham Brothers, Barry Docks in August 1963 and broken up by March 1965.

Marchwood Military Railway 0-6-0ST Hunslet No 3207

Name:	*Constantine (Arnhem)*
Manufacturer:	Hunslet Engine Co Ltd, Hunslet, Leeds
Built:	1945
Works number:	3207
Running numbers:	29 (LMR), 71443 and 157
At Marchwood:	1955 – 1958

This Hunslet version of the Austerity design was supplied new to the Longmoor Military Railway in 1945. It was to be named *Kitchener*, but this was never implemented – *Constantine* being applied in 1953. Its move to Marchwood came in November 1955, its time there lasting until November 1958, thereafter returning to Longmoor where it received another name change, this time to *Arnhem*. Its final years were spent as an exhibit until being sold for scrap to Pollock & Brown at Northam, Southampton in March 1968.

Marchwood Military Railway 0-4-0DM Andrew Barclay No 362

Name:	*Mulberry*
Manufacturer:	Andrew Barclay Sons & Co, Kilmarnock
Built:	1942
Works number:	362
Running numbers:	70047, 827 and 201
Engine:	153hp Gardner 6L3
Driving wheels:	3ft 3in
Wheelbase:	6ft 3in
Weight:	21ton 0cwt
At Marchwood:	1960 – 1965

Andrew Barclay No 362 was delivered new to the War Department in 1942 and sent to France during the Normandy campaign in 1944, returning to the UK in 1946. By January 1952 it was at Barby Ordnance Depot, near Rugby, then a month later it was off to Suez, returning to these shores and moving to Bicester in March 1955. After another spell at Barby it was transferred back to Bicester in September 1959. It remained there until February 1960 saw a move to Marchwood, where it took the name *Mulberry* in June 1962. A return to Bicester came in June 1965, followed by a move to Liphook Ordnance Depot in the following February. Under the 1968 scheme, it was renumbered Army 201 before yet another spell at Bicester from June 1970. By August 1971 it had arrived at Radway Green in Cheshire where it was renamed *Frog* and remained until rail traffic at the depot closed in October 1993. It was then privately purchased and taken to the Foxfield Railway before being handed over to the Stratford on Avon & Broadway Railway at the former MoD base at Long Marston in August 1996. There it has reverted to its former name *Mulberry*.

*"Foligno" in September 1959 suffers the indignity of being used for re-railing demonstrations at Longmoor.
(R.K. Blencowe Collection)*

*HE No 3207 as WD 157 at Marchwood on 22nd January 1956. Marchwood Power Station is under construction in
background. (D. Cull collection/KRM)*

Marchwood Military Railway 4wDM Ruston & Hornsby No 224348

Name:	*Pluto*
Manufacturer:	Ruston & Hornsby Ltd, Lincoln
Built:	1945
Works number:	224348
Running numbers:	72217 and 809
Engine:	48hp Ruston 4VRO
Driving wheels:	2ft 6in
Wheelbase:	5ft 2in
Weight:	6ton 0cwt
At Marchwood:	1962 – 1963

This Ruston shunter was supplied new to the War Department in 1945 and was sent to the Lockerley Stores Depot on the Hampshire Wiltshire border in March 1947. It then moved on to Bicester in July 1959 and by March 1962 it was at Marchwood, where it took the name *Pluto*. However, its duties there were short lived as it was back at Bicester early the next year. In January 1965 it was sold to Birds Commercial Motors Ltd at Long Marston, Worcester, then moving to Birds other premises at Pontymister in Glamorgan a year later. This was its final location as it was scrapped on site late in 1968.

Marchwood Military Railway 0-4-0DH North British No 27426

Name:	*Matruh*
Manufacturer:	North British Locomotive Co Ltd, Queens Park, Glasgow
Built:	1955
Works number:	27426
Running numbers:	8205 and 405
Engine:	275hp National
Driving wheels:	3ft 6in
Wheelbase:	6ft 0in
Weight:	32ton 0cwt
At Marchwood:	1962 – 1965, 1966 – 1968 and 1969 – 1974

This North British locomotive served three spells at Marchwood. After delivery to Bicester stores in April 1955 it was dispatched to Longmoor in February 1957 where it was given the name *Matruh* in 1959. Its first call at Marchwood came in June 1962, which lasted until being sent back to Bicester in May 1965. It worked on the Bicester Military Railway from September that year until moving back to Marchwood in June 1966. This second visit lasted until November 1968 when Bicester beckoned once more. Then in June the next year came the third and final call to Marchwood, which ended in November 1974 and included a trip to Andrew Barclay at Kilmarnock from June to August in 1973. Once again it was back to Bicester before moving to Longtown Ammunition Depot near Carlisle in July 1975. Five months later this much travelled engine was off to Donnington Ordnance Depot in Shropshire before its journey's end in Leuchars, Fife in July 1976 where it was given the name *River Tay*. At the end of active service in June 1989 it went to the nearby Lochty Private Railway, which closed in 1992, and was also with the Shropshire Locomotives Collection before purchase by S.A. Pye of Bramford, Ipswich where it is currently undergoing restoration.

Marchwood Military Railway 0-6-0DM Hunslet No 1846

Manufacturer:	Hunslet Engine Co Ltd, Hunslet, Leeds
Built:	1936
Works number:	1846
Running number:	855
Engine:	155hp Gardner 8L3
Driving wheels:	3ft 0in
Wheelbase:	8ft 0in
Weight:	22ton 0cwt
At Marchwood:	1965 – 1966

Hunslet No 1846 was supplied new to Corsham Ammunition Depot in Wiltshire, being one of a trio of locomotives with cut-down cabs for working underground. This loco spent several periods shuttling back and forth to Bicester until its home base faced imminent closure in the early 1960s. When it left Corsham for the last time in July 1962, again to Bicester, it was rebuilt to standard design before moving to West Moors Petroleum Storage Depot in Dorset in November 1963. By April 1965 it was at Marchwood where it spent a year before transfer back to Bicester. After becoming surplus to requirements in April 1968 it was sold to the Tunnel Portland Cement Company at Gartsherrie in Lanarkshire and finally scrapped around 1970.

Marchwood Military Railway 0-4-0DH North British No 27428

Manufacturer:	North British Locomotive Co Ltd, Queens Park, Glasgow
Built:	1955
Works number:	27428
Running numbers:	8207 and 407
Engine:	275hp National
Driving wheels:	3ft 6in
Wheelbase:	6ft 0in
Weight:	32ton 0cwt
At Marchwood:	1968 – 1975

Delivered new to Bicester in June 1955, this loco was placed in store until sent to Tidworth Vehicle depot in Wiltshire in January 1957. It remained there for a decade until it returned to Bicester in November 1967 before moving to Marchwood in August 1968. Apart from a trip to Andrew Barclay Sons & Co at Kilmarnock from February to June in 1973, its spell at the military port lasted until it returned to Bicester in July 1975, after which its final deployment was at Eskmeals Experimental Establishment in Cumberland from February 1976 until in March 1981. It was scrapped on site by Thomas W. Ward, of Barrow-in-Furness some six months later.

Marchwood Military Railway 0-4-0DH North British No 27422

Name:	*Salamander*
Manufacturer:	North British Locomotive Co Ltd, Queens Park, Glasgow
Built:	1955
Works number:	27422
Running numbers:	8201 and 401
Engine:	275hp National
Driving wheels:	3ft 6in
Wheelbase:	6ft 0in
Weight:	32ton 0cwt
At Marchwood:	1971 – 1973

Delivered new in April 1955 to the Royal Engineers at Kinnerley Junction on the Shropshire & Montgomeryshire Railway, North British No 27422 named *Salamander* saw eleven months service there before transfer to Tidworth vehicle depot in November of that year. Nine years later, in November 1964 came a move to Bicester until the following October brought a transfer to Long Marston. In May 1970 it was back to Bicester before arrival at Marchwood in October 1971. August 1973 saw the loco pay a visit to Andrew Barclay & Sons at Kilmarnock before returning to Long Marston in December of that year. Bicester beckoned once more in November 1975, a stay that lasted until its final duties brought a move to Ruddington Ordnance Factory in Nottingham in March 1979. It was finally disposed of in September 1981 to Track Supplies & Services of Wolverton, Buckinghamshire and was scrapped some six years later. For a picture of this locomotive, see page 66.

North British No 27422 as WD 8201 "Salamander" pictured in early days at Kinnerley loco shed on 16th August 1955.
(Brian Connell)

A rare steam sight in 1976 as "Waggoner" (HE No 3792/1953) hauls an internal stock passenger coach at a Marchwood public open day.
(Alan Thorpe)

Ruston No 459519 as Army 425 "River Tay" hauls an enthusiasts' train at Longmoor on 5th July 1969.
(R.K. Blencowe)

Marchwood Military Railway 0-6-0ST Hunslet No 3792

Name:	*Waggoner*
Manufacturer:	Hunslet Engine Co Ltd, Hunslet, Leeds
Built:	1953
Works number:	3792
Running numbers:	WD192 & 92
At Marchwood:	1973 – 1979

Hunslet No 3792 was one of the final batch of 14 Austerity saddle tanks delivered to the War Department in 1953, arriving at Longmoor in January that year. By July 1958 it had moved to Histon, but when that depot closed a year later another transfer took the loco to Bicester where it was placed into storage in May 1960. A year later it was at Long Marston, again in storage until moving to Shoeburyness in April 1969, by then renumbered as 92. A return to Long Marston came in June 1972 where it was given the name *Waggoner*. The following year saw its services required at Marchwood from June 1973, where it was needed to operate the internal passenger stock, which relied on a vacuum braking system. Its duties at the military port lasted until March 1979 when boiler repairs required a trip back to Shoeburyness. There it underwent a complete overhaul but was subsequently only used on odd occasions for VIP visits. In June 1984, *Waggoner* was sent to the Museum of Army Transport at Beverley. The National Army Museum took over responsibility in 2001 but two years later financial constraints brought closure and, once again the loco was placed in store until being loaned to the Isle of Wight Steam Railway in February 2005, where it joined fellow Austerity No 198 *Royal Engineer* and the preserved pair remain in active service.

Marchwood Military Railway 0-6-0DH Ruston & Hornsby No 459519

Name:	*River Tay*
Manufacturer:	Ruston & Hornsby Ltd, Lincoln
Built:	1961
Works number:	459519
Running numbers:	8219 & 425
TOPS number:	01507
Engine:	287hp Paxman 6RPH
Driving wheels:	3ft 6in
Wheelbase:	8ft 8in
Weight:	42ton 0cwt
At Marchwood:	1973 – 1986

Ruston No 459519 began its military career in July 1961 when arriving new at Ludgershall Vehicle depot in Wiltshire. A move to the Longmoor Railway came in November 1967 and by August 1969 it was at Long Marston. Following a visit to Bicester in May 1972 *River Tay* arrived at Marchwood in February 1973 and became one of the longest serving locos at the port before departing to Thomas Hill at Kilnhurst in March 1986. From there it passed to Longtown Ammunition Depot near Carlisle in October that year before departing for Air Force duty at Leuchars, Fife in August 1987. It remained there until transfer to Shoeburyness Experimental Establishment in May 1995 and by 2000 was stored at Bicester before moving to Ludgershall in November of that year. By September 2004 it had moved to the Royal Air Force at Caerwent in Gwent. It was finally sold out of service in June 2007 and, after a short stay at the Swanage Railway, it moved to Knights Rail Services at Eastleigh a month later.

Marchwood Military Railway 0-4-0DH North British No 27648

Manufacturer:	North British Locomotive Co Ltd, Queens Park, Glasgow
Built:	1959
Works number:	27648
Running numbers:	8213 & 413
Engine:	275hp National
Driving wheels:	3ft 6in
Wheelbase:	6ft 0in
Weight:	32ton 0cwt
At Marchwood:	1974 – 1976

This locomotive was delivered new to Kineton Ammunition Depot, Warwickshire in January 1959, seeing service there until being transferred to Bicester in March 1963. Over the next four years it made several trips back to Bicester's workshops before being sent to Ludgershall Vehicle Depot in November 1967. Its time there ended with a move to Marchwood in July 1974 which lasted until a return to Bicester in June 1976. After a visit to Andrew Barclay at Kilmarnock in April 1977 it returned to Ludgershall in February 1978, leaving there on a permanent transfer to the Royal Naval Armament Depot at Trecwn, Dyfed in August 1982. Its spell there ended in October 1994 when transferred to Long Marston, Warwickshire, where by 2000 it had been sold privately and is currently undergoing restoration.

Marchwood Military Railway 0-6-0DH Ruston & Hornsby No 466623

Manufacturer:	Ruston & Hornsby Ltd, Lincoln
Built:	1962
Works number:	466623
Running numbers:	8226 & 432
Engine:	287hp Paxman 6RPH
Driving wheels:	3ft 6in
Wheelbase:	8ft 8in
Weight:	42ton 0cwt
At Marchwood:	1974 – 1986

Long Marston Central Engineering Depot welcomed this loco new from the makers in January 1962, and it was off to Longtown Ammunition Depot, near Carlisle just three months later. In February 1963 it had arrived at Chilwell Ordnance Depot in Nottinghamshire, its long spell there ending in February 1972 with a move to Longtown Ammunition Depot in Cumbria. Ten months later it was at another ammunition depot, this time at Kineton in Warwickshire. A year later, in December 1973, it was at Bicester, and thence to Long Marston in June 1974. By October that year it was at Marchwood where it remained in service until June 1986 when transferred to Donnington Ordnance Depot in Shropshire. By 1994 it had returned to Kineton, moving to Ludgershall, Wiltshire in November 1995. A year later it was at Bicester until finally sent for scrap by J. Hirst & Sons at St. Mary Bourne, Whitchurch in January 2004.

Marchwood Military Railway 4wDH Rolls Royce No 10244

Manufacturer:	Rolls Royce Ltd, Sentinel Works, Shrewsbury
Built:	1966
Works number:	10244 (rebuilt as AB No 6528/1987)
Running numbers:	(244)
Engine:	255hp R-R C6SFL
Driving wheels:	3ft 2in
Wheelbase:	6ft 6in
Weight:	32ton 0cwt
At Marchwood:	1976 – 1979

This Rolls Royce loco was completed in July 1966 and delivered new to the Manchester ship Canal, working there until refurbishment by Thomas Hill (Rolls Royce's successors) at Kilnhurst in March 1972. The following April it was delivered to the MoD Air Force Depot at Quedgeley near Gloucester, where it was based until moving to Marchwood in August 1976. Another move came in March 1979 when it was transferred to RAF Chilmark in Wiltshire, where it carried the number 244. During its time there it was sent for rebuild at Andrew Barclay's works at Kilmarnock in December 1986, returning as AB No 6528 in June 1987. This was its final posting and its days ended when sent for scrap to Messrs. J. Hirst & Sons at St. Mary Bourne, Whitchurch in the summer of 1993.

Ludgershall was the location of North British No 27648/1959 as army No 413 on 26th July 1971. (Roger Hateley)

Ruston No 466623 as Army No 432 hauling Marchwood passenger stock on a public open day on 21st July 1979. (Lee Snelling)

Rolls Royce No 10244/1966 photographed at RAF Chilmark on 21st September 1989. (Robin Waywell)

Marchwood Military Railway 0-4-0DH North British No 27644

Manufacturer:	North British Locomotive Co Ltd, Queens Park, Glasgow
Built:	1959
Works number:	27644
Running numbers:	8209 & 409
Engine:	275hp National
Driving wheels:	3ft 6in
Wheelbase:	6ft 0in
Weight:	32ton 0cwt
At Marchwood:	1977 – 1979

This loco arrived at the Kineton Ammunition Depot in Warwickshire new from the makers in January 1959 and served there until transferred to Long Marston in April 1964. By December 1965, it was at Bicester until returning to Long Marston a year later. In November 1977 it became the last of the North British locos to serve at Marchwood in a duty that lasted until returning to Bicester in August 1979. Its final military role was played when the Eskmeals Experimental Establishment in Cumberland employed it from June 1980 until disposal to Marple & Gillot, Sheffield in July 1985. From there it went to the Tees Storage Co Ltd at Middlesborough in January 1986. It remained there until at least 1991 and is now privately owned and currently out of use at the Ayrshire Railway Preservation Society at Dalmellington.

Marchwood Military Railway 0-4-0DH North British No 27645

Manufacturer:	North British Locomotive Co Ltd, Queens Park, Glasgow
Built:	1958
Works number:	27645
Running numbers:	8210 and 410
Engine:	275hp National
Driving wheels:	3ft 6in
Wheelbase:	6ft 0in
Weight:	32ton 0cwt
At Marchwood:	1979 – 1980

North British No 27645 was delivered to Kineton Ammunition Depot, Warwickshire in December 1958 before moving to Bicester in August the following year. By June 1960 it had moved to Didcot Ordnance Depot where it remained for four years before transfer to Long Marston in February 1964. A further two years passed before a return to Bicester came in September 1966. The following year, a July move to Ruddington in Nottingham lasted a year before an onward journey to Yardley Chase in Northants materialised in July 1968. After a trip to Andrew Barclay at Kilmarnock in August 1967 the next port of call was the Bicester Military Railway in July 1978. Arrival at Marchwood came in August 1979, but in July 1980 a permanent allocation to Puriton, near Bridgewater in Somerset saw a decade of service there until sold to Mayer Newman & Co Ltd Snailwell, Cambridgeshire in mid-1990. It remains there today under current owners European Metal Recycling Ltd.

Marchwood Military Railway 0-6-0DH Ruston & Hornsby No 459518

Name:	*(Cromwell) (Churchill)*
Manufacturer:	Ruston & Hornsby Ltd, Lincoln
Built:	1961
Works number:	459518
Running numbers:	8217 and 423
Engine:	287hp Paxman 6RPH
Driving wheels:	3ft 6in
Wheelbase:	8ft 8in
Weight:	42ton 0cwt
At Marchwood:	1980 – 1985

Ruston No 459518 was supplied new to Bramley army depot in June 1961. After a visit to Bicester in July 1971 it returned to Bramley in October, remaining there until being sent to GEC Traction at Newton-le-Willows, Lancashire for overhaul in May 1979. It arrived at Marchwood in June 1980 where it had the distinction of once hauling a Royal Train. The next transfer came in March 1985 with a move to Shoeburyness, after which it found itself at Dean Hill Royal Naval Armament Depot on the Hampshire-Wiltshire border from August 1990 where it carried the name *Cromwell*. Its military service ended when declared surplus in March 2003, and it was privately purchased in May that year. The following month saw delivery to the Ecclesbourne Valley Railway at Wirksworth. Its most recent move came in February 2005 to the Great Central Railway at Ruddington where it has been renamed *Churchill*.

North British No 27644 resplendent as Army No 409 at Marchwood on 21st July 1979. (Lee Snelling)

North British No 27645/1959 pictured as army 8210 at Long Marston on 29th July 1974. (Roger Hateley)

Now carrying the name "Churchill" Ruston & Hornsby No 459518 enjoys retirement at Ruddington where it was pictured on 1st March 2005. (Jon Starkey)

Marchwood Military Railway 4wDH Thomas Hill No 310V

Name:	*Marchwood*
Manufacturer:	Thomas Hill (Rotherham) Ltd, Kilnhurst, Yorks
Built:	1984
Works number:	310V
Running number:	268
TOPS number:	01529
At Marchwood:	1984 – 1991 and 1992 – 2003

The aptly named *Marchwood* arrived new at its home base in March 1984 where, apart from a very brief trip to Bramley in January 1985, its only absence had been from October 1991 until February 1992 when it was away for overhaul at British Rail Engineering at Crewe. It then returned to Marchwood later that year and stayed until 2003 when transferred away. Its present home is the Ministry of Defence Munitions Depot at Kineton, Warwickshire.

Marchwood Military Railway 4wDH Thomas Hill No 311V

Name:	*McMullen*
Manufacturer:	Thomas Hill (Rotherham) Ltd, Kilnhurst, Yorks
Built:	1984
Works number:	311V
Running number:	269
TOPS number:	01530
At Marchwood:	1984 – 1991

McMullen was the second Thomas Hill loco at Marchwood, arriving in April 1984, remaining in service there until sent to British Rail Engineering at Crewe for overhaul in October 1991, having lost its name in 1988. On leaving there it was transferred to Longtown Ammunition Depot near Carlisle in January 1992. It was sent to the LH Group for a further overhaul in April 2004, leaving there five months later for the Royal Air Force at Caerwent, after which it had returned to Longtown by September 2007.

Marchwood Military Railway 4wDH Thomas Hill No 308V

Name:	*Mulberry*
Manufacturer:	Thomas Hill (Rotherham) Ltd, Kilnhurst, Yorks
Built:	1983
Works number:	308V
Running number:	266
TOPS number:	01547
At Marchwood:	1985 – 1986 and 1986 – 1992

Mulberry began life at Long Marston when new from Thomas Hill in November 1983, but by December the following year was with the Royal Air Force at Caerwent in Gwent. However, it was back at Long Marston in January 1985 before coming to Marchwood two months later. Apart from a brief two month visit to Moreton-on-Lugg ordnance depot between April and June 1986, no more travels were encountered until January 1992 saw it go to British Rail Engineering at Crewe for overhaul. By 1994 it had moved to East Riggs, Dumfries until its stay in Scotland ended in July 2000 with a transfer to Longtown ammunition depot in Cumbria. In August 2003 it was sent to the LH Group for overhaul before moving on to Kineton in Warwickshire in October 2003, where it is still in service.

Army No 268 (Thomas Hill No 310V/1984) pictured at Marchwood on 16th October 1989. (Robin Waywell)

Another of the Thomas Hill brigade at Marchwood. This time No 311V/1984 as army No 269 on 16th October 1989. (Robin Waywell)

Marchwood Military Railway 4wDH Thomas Hill No 298V

Name:	(*Sapper*) (*Mulberry*)
Manufacturer:	Thomas Hill (Rotherham) Ltd, Kilnhurst, Yorks
Built:	1981
Works number:	298V
Running number:	258
TOPS number:	01549
At Marchwood:	1988 – 1989 and 1999 – 2004

Thomas Hill No 298V was delivered new to Bicester Military Railway in November 1981. From May 1985 until January 1988 it carried the name *Sapper*, but this had disappeared by the time it came to Marchwood in April 1988. Following a brief return to Bicester between March and May the following year it moved to Ludgershall in September 1989. By July 1990 it had moved to Moreton-on–Lugg ordnance depot in Herefordshire, thence to Caerwent Air Force depot in Gwent in December 1990, and on to Longtown, near Carlisle in April 1991. In November 1999 it was back at Marchwood carrying the name *Mulberry* before an overhaul by the LH Group in November 2004. After this, it returned to Caerwent in March 2005, where it lost its latest name, and remains there today.

Marchwood Military Railway 4wDH Thomas Hill No 303V

Name:	*McMullen*
Manufacturer:	Thomas Hill (Rotherham) Ltd, Kilnhurst, Yorks
Built:	1982
Works number:	303V
Running number:	263
TOPS number:	01543
At Marchwood:	1990 – 2004

Not to be confused with the other *McMullen* (Thomas Hill No 311V which carried that name until 1988) No 303V was delivered by the makers to the Ludgershall Vehicle Depot, Wiltshire, in August 1982. By July 1990 it was at BR Engineering at Crewe for an overhaul, following which it arrived at Marchwood in November that year. Its stay lasted until February 2004 when it went to the LH Group for another overhaul, following which it moved to Kineton ammunition depot where it remains today.

Marchwood Military Railway 4wDH Thomas Hill No 273V

Name:	*Mulberry*
Manufacturer:	Thomas Hill (Rotherham) Ltd, Kilnhurst, Yorks
Built:	1977
Works number:	273V
Running number:	255
TOPS number:	01546
At Marchwood:	1991 – 2003

Service life for this loco began when it was delivered new to Kineton Ammunition Depot in Warwickshire in August 1977. Nine years elapsed before a transfer to the Royal Air Force at Chilmark, Wiltshire came in August 1985. Next stop was Ludgershall Vehicle Depot in July 1990 before moving to the Navy depot at Bedenham, Gosport just two months later. June 1991 saw a visit to BR Engineering at Crewe and, after an overhaul, it came to Marchwood in October that year, being stationed there until 2003. Its current posting is at Kineton Ammunitions Depot in Warwickshire.

Army No 263 was one of the earlier Thomas Hill locos (303V/1982) and was photographed at Ludgershall on 15th May 1989. (Robin Waywell)

Thomas Hill No 273V/1977 carried the name "Mulberry" at Marchwood, where it was pictured on 24th June 1995. (Roger Hateley)

Marchwood Military Railway 4wDH Thomas Hill No 274V

Name:	*Marlborough*
Manufacturer:	Thomas Hill (Rotherham) Ltd, Kilnhurst, Yorks
Built:	1977
Works number:	274V
Running number:	256
TOPS number:	01527
At Marchwood:	1991 – 2000 and 2003 – present day

Marlborough was delivered new to the Kineton Ammunitions Depot in October 1977, moving to Donnington Ordnance Depot, Shropshire, in October in 1989. A transfer to Bicester's workshops came in April 1991, before an overhaul at BR's works at Crewe some two months later. By October 1991 it had arrived at Marchwood where it remained until moving back to Bicester in 2000, staying there before overhaul at the LH Group in April 2003. In October that year it was back at Marchwood where it is still currently in service.

Marchwood Military Railway 0-4-0DM Fowler No 22503

Name:	*Percy*
Manufacturer:	John Fowler & Co (Leeds) Ltd, Hunslet, Leeds
Built:	1938
Works number:	22503
Running numbers:	815 and Army 111
Engine:	60hp
Driving wheels:	3ft 0in
Wheelbase:	5ft 6in
Weight:	15ton 0cwt
At Marchwood:	1993 – present day

This veteran Fowler diesel made its debut in 1938 when it was new to the War Department at Asfordby Experimental Establishment, near Melton Mowbray in Leicestershire. It was renumbered Army 111 in 1968 and moved to Bicester in July 1969. In October 1973 it was shipped off to Monchengladbach, Germany where it was put on display at the headquarters of the Royal Corps of Transport's 79 Railway Squadron. Given the name *Percy* it served as a static exhibit until returning home to the UK in 1993 and is now at Marchwood where it remains in preservation.

Marchwood Military Railway 4wDH Thomas Hill No 275V

Name:	*(Tela) Mexeflote*
Manufacturer:	Thomas Hill (Rotherham) Ltd, Kilnhurst, Yorks
Built:	1978
Works number:	275V
Running number:	257
TOPS number:	01548
At Marchwood:	1999 – 2003 and 2004 – present day

Yet another of the Thomas Hill Vanguard locos built for the military, No 275V arrived at Bicester Ordnance depot from the makers in June 1978 bearing the name *Tela*. By November that year it had been dispatched to Longtown Ammunition Depot near Carlisle, where it stayed until moving on to the Kineton Depot in Warwickshire in January 1981. Another move, this time to the engineers at nearby Long Marston came in June 1990, after which it was sent to the Royal Navy Armament Depot at Trecwn, Dyfed in January 1994. Its journey then continued to Ludgershall, Wiltshire in the following September, and in 1999 it came to Marchwood. It was dispatched to the LH Group for overhaul in September 2003, returning to Marchwood in 2004 where it has remained to the present day and carries the name *Mexeflote*.

Army No 256 "Marlborough" (Thomas Hill 274V/1977) on duty at Marchwood on 24th June 1995. (Roger Hateley)

Marchwood Military Railway 4wDH Thomas Hill No 300V

Manufacturer:	Thomas Hill (Rotherham) Ltd, Kilnhurst, Yorks
Built:	1982
Works number:	300V
Running number:	260
TOPS number:	01541
At Marchwood:	2003 – present day

New from Thomas Hill in 1982, this loco went directly to Long Marston in April that year, remaining for eight years before the need for overhaul took it to BR at Crewe in April 1990. On return to service in June that year it was transferred to Ludgershall. After moving to the Bicester Military Railway in Oxfordshire in 1994 there followed another onward transfer to Kineton Ammunition Depot, Warwickshire in the following year. Then it was back to Bicester's RE workshops at Arncott sometime in the mid to late 1990s, remaining there until being sent to the LH Group for overhaul in April 2003. It came to Marchwood later that year and is still resident. .

Marchwood Military Railway 4wDH Thomas Hill No 301V

Manufacturer:	Thomas Hill (Rotherham) Ltd, Kilnhurst, Yorks
Built:	1982
Works number:	301V
Running number:	261
TOPS number:	01524
At Marchwood:	2004 and 2005 – present day

This loco made its debut at the Aldershot Military Display in June 1982 before being stationed at Long Marston in the same month. Little else happened until the need for overhaul saw a trip to BR at Crewe in April 1990. Three months later it was back in service at Ludgershall. This loco found its way to Marchwood in 2004 before being sent away to the LH Group for overhaul and returning to Marchwood again in 2005 where it remains at present.

MoD loco No 261 (No 301V/1982) heads a trio of Thomas Hill locos at Ludgershall camp shed on 5th October 1994. The others are 264 (No 306V/1983) and 257 (No 275V/1978). (Dave Purvis)

Hythe Pier Railway 1909 – Present Day

The Hythe Pier Railway has been written about and photographed countless times – and rightly so, as this relic of a bygone era retains all the charm and history of a time when speed and comfort were not always high on life's agenda.

The pier itself was constructed in iron during 1879/80 and opened to the public on 1st January 1881 at a cost of £7,700 by the grandly named Hythe Pier and Hythe and Southampton Ferry Company. Because of the high level of tidal mud, it needed to reach out some 2100 feet where deeper water allowed the vessels easier and more frequent transit for passengers travelling by ferry across the River Test to Southampton. In its first year of operation, some 124,533 members of the public had passed over it.

The original plans for the 16ft wide structure included a railway down the centre of the pier. However, the 2ft gauge tracks were not installed until 1909 and were eventually positioned along the south side, allowing a wider promenade for foot passengers (and the occasional carriage?), while additional sidings were added during the following year. At this time traffic was limited to hand propelled, solid wheeled luggage trolleys.

The biggest innovation came when an electric passenger tramway was laid down in 1922 with further sidings, one for stock and another into the workshop. A new ticket office replaced the old tollhouse at the landward end. Three locomotives built by Brush for a WWI Avonmouth Mustard Gas factory were purchased in July that year. These were battery operated at 100 volts but were adapted to take a 200 volt current from a third rail (on the south side of track away from passengers with a fence separating them from the railway). The current (subsequently 240v) was fed from a small generating station near the toll house. The vintage passenger stock consists of three unsprung two-bogie coaches built by the Drury Car Company and can carry up to 48 passengers.

In 1923 the company changed its name to the more simplified title of Hythe Pier Co Ltd and in 1947 the pier head was reconstructed to allow easier access to vessels. Another major modernisation took place in 1970/71 under the General Estates Company.

The pier, ferries and railway are currently operated by White Horse Ferries, who suffered a crisis in November 2003 when a drunken captain ran his dredger through a section of the pier, creating a gaping hole in the decking and the railway. Despite such serious damage, the pier was open for business again in January 2004 and this delightful antiquity continues to charm young and old alike.

An early image of the Hythe Pier taken before the railway was laid down in 1909. Note the hand trucks for passenger's luggage. (Bert Moody Collection)

Hythe Pier in 1913 with the paddle steamer "Hampton" alongside. The railway then consisted of hand propelled luggage trolleys. (Author's Collection)

Hythe Pier and the now electrified train pictured in 1931. Note the engine is unusually facing the seaward end of the railway. (Bert Moody Collection)

Little has changed on the railway since this photo of the Hythe Pier train approaching the landward station was taken around 1950. (Author's Collection)

Hythe Pier 4wRE Brush No 16302

Manufacturer:	Brush Electrical Engineering Co Ltd, Loughborough
Built:	1917
Works number:	16302 (on engine casing)
Engine:	240v DC
Driving wheels:	1ft 4in
Gauge:	2ft 0in
At Hythe:	1922 – present day

One of four Brush-built locomotives built in 1917 for use in a Ministry of Munitions mustard gas factory at Avonmouth. When the factory closed in 1921 the locos were sold off, with three of them going to Hythe Pier in 1922. This engine has seen over eight decades of service and still going strong.

Hythe Pier 4wBE Brush No 16304

Manufacturer:	Brush Electrical Engineering Co Ltd, Loughborough
Built:	1917
Works number:	16304 (on engine casing)
Engine:	100v Batteries
Driving wheels:	1ft 4in
Gauge:	2ft 0in
At Hythe:	1922

This member of the ex-Avonmouth fleet arrived with two of its sisters at Hythe in 1922. Unlike the others, it was never converted to 200v 3rd-rail power, being dismantled and used as spare parts for the other two.

One of the three Brush locos in its original form as battery driven pictured at the Avonmouth mustard gas factory when new. (Bert Moody Collection)

Hythe Pier loco pictured on 7th June 2004 after repairs to the pier.
(I.J. Bovey)

Hythe Pier 4wRE Brush No 16307

Manufacturer:	Brush Electrical Engineering Co Ltd, Loughborough
Built:	1917
Works number:	16307 (on engine casing)
Engine:	240v
Driving wheels:	1ft 4in
Gauge:	2ft 0in
At Hythe:	1922 – present day

This loco from Avonmouth arrived at Hythe with the two others in 1922. Together with its surviving sister it has provided unbroken service for pier passengers since that time

One of the two Hythe Pier locos stands at the workshops after refurbishment on 3rd May 2005.
(I.J. Bovey)

The tracks inside the Polimeri works on 10th May 2007, with the siding to the loco shed on the left. (Author)

The disused sidings, facing west, at the factory loading bay on 10th May 2007. (Author)

CHAPTER 12

International Synthetic Rubber Company Hythe 1957 – 1985

The rail sidings at the ISR Co were laid down in 1957, when the firm's Ruston loco was delivered new by road. The initial use of the sidings was to bring in materials to assist in building the company plant, and rail movements were carried out by contractor Matthew Hall, but once the factory was up and running, operation of the system passed to ISR.

Once inside the company premises, the twin tracks run parallel for some 400 yards, serving two loading bays and a weighbridge. A return siding leads back to the loco shed where the Ruston shunter is still housed. The loco had two water boxes fitted to its exhaust system to act as a spark arrester in keeping with the factory requirements at the time.

A number of materials for the production process arrived by rail on the Totton to Fawley line and were transferred to the sidings by BR loco. Some of the finished products were then assembled for rail collection and distribution, to both national and international markets. Rail traffic significantly reduced around 1967 when the use of pallets and road transport took over, however, a small number of raw materials were still delivered to the site by rail until approximately 1985. The firm of Enichem UK Ltd subsequently took over the site and current owner and operator of the plant is Polimeri Europa UK Ltd, who continue to manufacture synthetic rubber and related products.

The sidings still exist, although the points connection to the main line was cut in 2004. The unused tracks are in reasonable condition, but Polimeri have no plans for a return to rail transport and the loco remains stored in its shed, in an unserviceable condition, with its future undecided.

The ISR Ruston stands silently inside the loco shed at Hythe on 10th May 2007. (Author)

International Synthetic Rubber 4wDM Ruston & Hornsby No 416568

Manufacturer:	Ruston & Hornsby Ltd, Lincoln
Built:	1957
Works number:	416568
Engine:	88hp Ruston 4VPO
Driving wheels:	3ft 0in
Wheelbase:	5ft 10in
Weight:	17ton 0cwt
At Hythe:	1957 – present day (currently out of use)

Ruston No 416568 was completed by the makers in November 1957 and delivered new to contractors Matthew Hall who were engaged in building a factory for the International Synthetic Rubber Factory at Hythe, near Southampton. After completion of the works, operation of the rail system passed to the owners until it fell out of use in 1985. Since that date the loco has been stored on site in the locomotive shed.

The Hythe ISR Ruston pictured during one of its last ventures outside the loco shed. (Enichem UK Ltd)

CHAPTER 13

Fawley Refinery 1920 – Present Day

Building a refinery on marshlands at Fawley presented many difficulties in a remote area with no rail access and very poor roads. However, in August 1920 the Anglo Gulf West Indies Petroleum Corporation (AGWI) set about this onerous task. Through the agency of Sir J.F. Payne Gallway, Brown and Co Ltd, a site at the Burt Boulton and Haywood premises at Totton was set up to receive materials and stores via the Eling tramway. These would be carried on barges down to the quay at Ashlett Creek. Contractor B. Whittaker & Sons of Leeds was appointed to carry out the works, and their first undertaking was to construct a narrow gauge railway from the quay at Ashlett Creek to the nearby refinery site. One of the early consignments landed there included a steam locomotive and 22 side tipping wagons, plus a vertical boiler, temporary electric lighting gear, concrete mixing equipment and a number of pumps. The barges were unloaded by a standard gauge rail mounted steam crane onto 2ft gauge wagons, at first propelled by horses, but very soon by the locomotive.

Whittaker made use of a Wren class Kerr Stuart 0-4-0ST, thought to be No 4018 built in 1919, which arrived in the early days of construction. The first stage of construction was completed by June 1921 when the initial vessel carrying crude oil docked at the quay. At this time, the loco was transferred to AGWI ownership and was soon joined by an 0-4-0T No 123 built in 1891 by the continental firm of Decauville. The pair were housed in a small loco shed on the refinery site.

By August 1922, Whittaker had taken delivery of a small petrol loco, this being Motor Rail, No 426 built in 1917. 4-wheel engines such as this had been commonly in use on military lines during WWI, and large numbers were surplus to requirements after hostilities ceased. Whittaker is noted as having two more of these (numbers 433 and 1296, both also of 1917 vintage) but there is no record of them being used at Fawley.

Early stages of construction with concrete piles mounted on wooden trolleys for transportation from Ashlett Creek. (Esso Petroleum Co)

First steps in 1920 as the contractor's line reaches out across the marshes to a steam pile driver.
(E. Mudge/KRM collection)

The Decauville loco with a train of spoil tip wagons during the construction of the Fawley site. (Esso Petroleum Co)

In 1923, AGWI expanded their operations with the building of an asphalt plant. The increased activity placed greater demands on the railway and Motor Rail No 426 was taken into AGWI ownership that year, being their third loco and taking the running number H.3.

By 1926, a passenger service had been established on the refinery railway, ferrying personnel between the works and the jetty on some very basic seated wagons. By the end of that year, AGWI had purchased a second Motor Rail loco (No 463 built in 1917), this became H.4.

The following year saw three more arrivals, again from Motor Rail, these being numbers H.5, H.6 and H.7. Few details of this trio are known, except that one of them was Motor Rail No 3839, built in 1926. This sudden influx of petrol locos coincided with the demise of the two steam engines, both of which are thought to have been taken away by sea in 1927. Another casualty was Motor Rail H.3, which disappeared around the same time.

The Totton Hythe & Fawley branch line had opened in 1925 after which a connection was made to the refinery. AGWI's first standard gauge loco was acquired new from Motor Rail in 1927; this was No 4169, becoming H.8 on arrival. To accommodate it, a new two road shed was built with one track of each gauge.

A further batch of narrow gauge Motor Rail locos arrived in 1928. These were numbers H.9, H.10, H.11 and H.12, and all were supplied new from the maker. There is no record of the works numbers, but H.10 appears in the refinery archives as serial No 49/5180 and H.12 as No 7824, neither of which matches any Motor Rail documents. A year later, one of the earlier models, No 463 (H.4) was sold to a contractor in Aberdeen.

By 1929 the works had undergone another expansion, this time under AGWI's successors, the Anglo American Oil Company (the UK arm of Esso Petroleum). A new jetty had been added to the refinery and the increased traffic now avoided Ashlett Creek, though the quay was still used up until the Second World War.

There were no further comings and goings until No 1252 turned up new from Motor Rail in 1933 as H.13, and it was another two years before the refinery took possession of its second standard gauge loco, this being yet another Motor Rail in the form of No 3896, delivered new in 1935 and becoming H.14. The next Motor Rail, No 4702, was delivered second hand from the makers in September 1937 as H.15, having been with the manufacturer's hire subsidiary since new in 1934. Its appearance sparked another cull of older models as H.5, H.6 and H.7 were scrapped.

Not built for comfort (or safety) this refinery passenger vehicle was still in evidence when photographed on 3rd June 1950. (John A. Bailey/Bert Moody collection)

Barrels galore, with the refinery still expanding. This picture shows the narrow gauge tracks evident in the centre of the photo and a standard gauge train at the rear. (E. Mudge/KRM collection)

The refinery continues to grow as this scene shows an Anglo American bitumen wagon (bottom right) while a narrow gauge train is silhouetted in the distance. (E. Mudge/KRM collection)

On now to 1938, when Motor Rail No 4716 of 1936 (H.16) came via the same route, with the final narrow gauge Motor Rail No 4724 (H.17) arriving new in 1939. During the dark days of the World War Two, production at the refinery was run down with very little activity until peace returned once again. H.10 had been disposed of in 1943 and at the war's end the loco count was nine – two standard and seven narrow gauge. There were no further disposals until H.11 "met its maker" in 1948, a year that also saw an order for the refinery's final Motor Rail loco, No 5755. This was a standard gauge model delivered new from the makers in January 1949 but never allocated a number in the H series. It was also the last loco to arrive at the "old" refinery, where big changes were afoot.

By the time Motor Rail No 5755 had arrived, plans were already in the air to enlarge the refinery. The huge new works expansion began in July 1949 employing over 5,000 contract workers, and was completed in September 1951 at a cost of £37.5m, some four months ahead of schedule. During this period, a number of 3ft gauge Hibberd "Planet" diesels belonging to Danish contractors Christiani & Nielsen, were on site from 1950, where they were engaged in the construction of the refinery's new jetties. There were at least four such locos, and possibly a fifth engaged in this work.

When officially opened by Prime Minister Clement Atlee in September 1951, Fawley (now under new banner of Esso Petroleum) was the largest oil refinery in Europe, processing up to 5.5 million gallons of oil each day. The new jetties now received much larger tankers and the facilities at Ashlett Creek became redundant, while the internal narrow gauge railway was rundown until finally closed in 1961. All but three of the remaining Motor Rail locos had been disposed of by 1957. The standard gauge No 5755 and narrow gauge No 3896 were both sold in 1960, leaving No 4724 as the last remnant of the narrow gauge. Its final duties were to assist in the dismantling of the abandoned system, including materials on the old AGWI jetty, before being handed over to the Hampshire Narrow Gauge Railway Society for preservation.

An aerial view of the refinery taken at the time of its expansion works in 1951. (Southampton City Archive)

In the years after its completion, much of the colossal output from the refinery was to be transported by rail, and a new yard for marshalling the traffic was constructed adjacent to the main line in 1950. In January of that year, a large American 0-4-4-0DE locomotive (GEU No 30483/1949) was shipped over and employed in the construction of a new three and a half mile branch line into the refinery, this being completed within six months. Greater locomotive power was soon required and, in 1953 and 1955, two North British 0-4-0DH locos arrived (numbers 27078 and 27415 respectively), these were followed in 1963 by an 0-6-0DH English Electric shunter (No 8423) and a Rolls Royce 4-wheel DH (No 10197) in 1976.

The 0-4-4-0 "Yank" was disposed of in May 1978, passing to the Steamtown Museum, Carnforth, while the refinery saw the arrivals of two 0-6-0DH Hunslets, No 7542 appeared in 1978, as a direct replacement for its American cousin, and No 8999 followed in 1981, while a third Hunslet, No 8998 arrived in 1985. The three Hunslet locos received names as a result of an Esso staff competition and bore the plates *Greenfinch*, *Redwing* and *Bluebird*, each being painted in the appropriate livery. A Thomas Hill loco, No 285V, was on loan to Fawley for six months in 1999 while HE 8999 was away for repair.

The refinery has continued to grow and covers some 3,200 acres, processing over 10 million gallons per day, but now 85 percent of the oil is transported by pipeline, and another 10 percent by sea; only a small percentage is handled by rail or road. In the 1970s there were up to 40 rail movements daily but the remaining traffic is now just two or three arrivals and departures each day. These are composed mainly of bitumen trains to Birmingham and Plymouth. some cargoes of Gas Oil to various train operators, and a small amount of crude. This decline has reduced the locomotive requirements and only two engines are now needed to handle the small amount of rail traffic, the fleet having been reduced when No 7542 was scrapped in December 2003. The most recent recruit has been Hunslet/Barclay 0-6-0DH No 659, appearing from April 2006 until April 2008 as a replacement for both HEs (numbers 8999 and 8998), which were successively sent away for overhaul.

There is now little sign of the old refinery, although the original AGWI jetty remains in a dilapidated state with the rails still in place. Other remnants from the old system are still evident in a few places, while the dual gauge loco shed still retains the narrow gauge inspection pit.

The remains of the original AGWI jetty at Fawley on 15th April 2008, where subsidence at the landward end has somewhat distorted the old narrow gauge tracks. (Author)

FAWLEY REFINERY 1920 – PRESENT DAY

Right: This photo taken from an Esso booklet published in 1951 shows the American 0-4-4-0DE General Electric loco No 30483 working on the newly constructed refinery branch line.

Below: The "Yank" picks its way through the construction debris in 1950. (Southampton City Archive)

Left: Traces of the original AGWI narrow gauge system are evident in when looking back along the old Jetty Road. (Author)

Below: The railways at Fawley Refinery in 1938, showing the complex narrow gauge system and the later standard gauge tracks from the main line sidings. (Map by Roger Hateley)

FAWLEY OLD REFINERY 1938

Stores

Jetty Road

To jetty

Main Road

Power House Rd

Power House

Workshops

Loco Shed

Old Loco Shed

Copthorne Lane

To Ashlett Creek

0   100
YARDS

jetty

Fawley Station

Refinery

Ashlett Creek

Fawley Refinery 0-4-0ST Kerr, Stuart No 4018

Manufacturer:	Kerr, Stuart & Co Ltd, California Works, Stoke on Trent
Built:	1919
Works number:	4018
Running numbers:	H1 (AGWI)
Cylinders:	6in x 9in
Driving wheels:	1ft 8in
Wheelbase:	3ft 0in
Working pressure:	140psi
Water capacity:	87gals
Weight:	4ton 5cwt
Gauge:	2ft 0in
At Fawley:	1921 – 1927

Few precise details are known of this "Wren" class loco's identity but what little evidence there is suggests it may be as above. Many such engines were purchased as war surplus and this one possibly came from Porton Military Camp in Wiltshire when purchased by contractor B. Whittaker & Sons of Leeds during the early years of the refinery construction. It was first recorded at Fawley in 1921 and taken into AGWI stock during the following year when joined by an 0-4-0 Decauville tank.

Its days at the refinery came to an end in 1927 when, having been replaced by petrol driven locos, it was believed to have been sold, along with the Decauville engine, to dealer William Jones of Greenwich. It was last heard of when working for contractor D. Mackenzie & Co of Shirley, Birmingham in 1945 and nothing further is recorded.

Fawley Refinery 0-4-0T Decauville No 123

Manufacturer:	Decauville S.A. Corbeil, Paris
Built:	1891
Works number:	123
Running numbers:	2 (Kensal Gasworks), H2 (AGWI)
Cylinders:	7in x 9.75in
Driving wheels:	1ft 11.5in
Weight:	5ton 0cwt
Gauge:	2ft 0in
At Fawley:	1922 – 1927

Information about this loco is slightly more forthcoming than that of its Kerr, Stuart partner at Fawley, and its identity is thought to be as above. No 123 was purchased new by the Gas Light & Coke Company at Kensal Green Gasworks in London as their No 2 engine and was requisitioned by the Government in 1916. After the First World War it was deemed surplus at Chitterne Dump in Wiltshire, and was purchased by AGWI in 1922. Its time at Fawley lasted until it was sold in 1927 to dealer William Jones of Greenwich, and was later used by Oxford Corporation during the construction of the Wolvercote section of the Oxford Northern Bypass during 1931–32. No further details are known of its eventual demise.

Decauville No 123 at work on the Oxford Northern Bypass contract on 14th June 1931.
(Dr J. R. Hollick)

Fawley Refinery 4wPM Motor Rail No 426

Manufacturer:	Motor Rail Ltd, Simplex Works, Bedford
Built:	1917
Works number:	426
Running numbers:	WDLR 2147 (War Department), H3 (AGWI)
Engine:	40hp Dorman 4JO
Driving wheels:	1ft 6in
Wheelbase:	4ft 0in
Weight:	6ton 15cwt
Gauge:	2ft 0in
At Fawley:	1922 – 1927

Motor Rail No 426 was delivered new to the Military in February 1917 as WDLR No 2147 and served in France as one of the "protected", and later "armoured" types. Like so many other wartime locomotives it was sold off at the end of hostilities, possibly from the dump at Beauraineville from where it was purchased through agents Sir J.F. Payne, Gallway Brown & Co Ltd for contractor B. Whittaker & Son who employed it on the refinery construction from 1922. After being transferred to AGWI in 1923 it worked on until being scrapped in 1927.

Fawley Refinery 4wPM Motor Rail No 463

Manufacturer:	Motor Rail Ltd, Simplex Works, Bedford
Built:	1917
Works number:	463
Running numbers:	WDLR 2184 (War Department), H4 (AGWI)
Engine:	40hp Dorman 4JO
Driving wheels:	1ft 6in
Wheelbase:	4ft 0in
Weight:	6ton 15cwt
Gauge:	2ft 0in
At Fawley:	1926 – 1929

This was an armoured version of the Motor Rail locomotive and was supplied to the War Department Light Railways during WWI. Motor Rail No 463 was delivered to the Military in February 1917 as WDLR 2184 for service in France, and when hostilities ended it was sold off as surplus to government requirements. By December 1926 it had been purchased by AGWI from contractor James Byrom Ltd, Bury but it remained at Fawley for only a short period before being moved on to contractor William Tawse Ltd of Aberdeen in November 1929 for whom it was later recorded as in use for aerodrome defence works during the Second World War, and is presumed scrapped soon afterwards.

Motor Rail No 463/1917 was one of the armoured versions of the Simplex loco and is pictured during its wartime service in France.
(Lens of Sutton)

Fawley Refinery 4wPM Motor Rail No 3839

Manufacturer:	Motor Rail Ltd, Simplex Works, Bedford
Built:	1926
Works number:	3839 (previously Motor Rail numbers 397 and 2231)
Running numbers:	H5 (AGWI)
Engine:	40hp Dorman 4JO
Driving wheels:	1ft 6in
Wheelbase:	4ft 0in
Weight:	6ton 0cwt
Gauge:	2ft 0in
At Fawley:	1927 – 1937

This is one of a trio of Motor Rail locos supplied to AGWI in 1927, the numbers of the other two not being known. It was originally built in July 1917 as Motor Rail No 397 for use by the Ministry of Munitions in France. Following disposal after the war, it was reconstructed in 1923 as No 2231 and became the property of contractors Stewart McDonnell of Tolworth near Surbiton in January 1924. Another reconstruction in 1926 saw it emerge as No 3839, being dispatched to Fawley in January 1927. Nothing much else is known other than it was sold off with the other two in 1937.

Fawley Refinery 4wPM Motor Rail

Manufacturer:	Motor Rail Ltd, Simplex Works, Bedford
Built:	1926
Works number:	Not known
Running numbers:	H6 (AGWI)
Engine:	40hp
Driving wheels:	1ft 6in
Wheelbase:	4ft 0in
Gauge:	2ft 0in
At Fawley:	1927 – 1937

This loco is the second of the of Motor Rail trio of locos supplied to AGWI in 1927, one of then being No 3839. Few other details are recorded other than it was sold off with the other two in 1937.

Fawley Refinery 4wPM Motor Rail

Manufacturer:	Motor Rail Ltd, Simplex Works, Bedford
Built:	1926
Works number:	Not known
Running numbers:	H7 (AGWI)
Engine:	40hp
Driving wheels:	1ft 6in
Wheelbase:	4ft 0in
Gauge:	2ft 0in
At Fawley:	1927 – 1937

This loco is the third of the unidentified trio of trio of Motor Rail locos supplied to AGWI in 1927, one of which was No 3839. Little else is recorded other than it was sold off with the other two in 1937.

Fawley Refinery 4wPM Motor Rail No 4169

Manufacturer:	Motor Rail Ltd, Simplex Works, Bedford
Built:	1926
Works number:	4169 (previously 2263 built early 1920s)
Running numbers:	H8 (AGWI)
Engine:	65hp
Weight:	16ton 0cwt
At Fawley:	1927 – 1957

This loco began life in the 1920s as Motor Rail No 2263 before being renumbered to 4169 when rebuilt in December 1926. Arriving at Fawley in March 1927 it was one of only three standard gauge Motor Rail locos supplied to the AGWI refinery. It was converted to diesel in October 1939 and, in contrast to some of its sister engines, its stay was quite prolonged, remaining at Fawley for some 30 years before being sold on to dealers Joseph Pugsley & Sons Ltd at Stoke Gifford, Gloucester in 1957. It was recorded as purchased by Shakespere Simpson & Cook, at New Brickwood, Somercoates, Derbyshire in April 1959. Further records show the loco was back with Pugsley & Sons who advertised it for sale in February 1961, but no further owner is known and it is possible it ended its days there.

Motor Rail No 4169 (with Motor Rail No 5755 on the left) at the refinery shed on 3rd June 1950. (John A. Bailey/Bert Moody Collection)

Fawley Refinery 4wPM Motor Rail

Manufacturer:	Motor Rail Ltd, Simplex Works, Bedford
Built:	Not known
Works number:	Not known
Running numbers:	H9 (AGWI)
Engine:	20hp
Gauge:	2ft 0in
At Fawley:	1928 – 1957

This loco is a Fawley mystery, with no details other than it being another of the host of narrow gauge Motor Rail engines to work at the refinery. Its original details are not recorded, but having arrived there from the makers in 1928 it saw lengthy service until disposed of for scrap in 1957.

Fawley Refinery 4wPM Motor Rail No 7824

Manufacturer:	Motor Rail Ltd, Simplex Works, Bedford
Built:	Not known
Works number:	Not known
Running numbers:	H12, N.L.3 (both AGWI)
Engine:	20hp
Gauge:	2ft 0in
At Fawley:	1928 – 1957

This Motor Rail loco was one of four engines supplied by the makers to Fawley refinery in 1928. Its number is shown in the Esso archives as 7824 but this does not correspond with any of the manufacturer's records. Its duties at the refinery lasted until 1957 when it was disposed of and presumed scrapped.

Fawley Refinery 4wPM Motor Rail No 49/5180

Manufacturer:	Motor Rail Ltd, Simplex Works, Bedford
Built:	Not known
Works number:	Not known
Running numbers:	H10 (AGWI)
Engine:	20hp
Gauge:	2ft 0in
At Fawley:	1928 – 1943

Another mystery loco in the Fawley Motor Rail fleet, having been supplied by the makers in 1928. The odd serial number is one that was recorded in the Esso Petroleum Co records and does not relate to anything in the Motor Rail files. After survival into the Second World War years it was disposed of in 1943 and presumed scrapped.

Fawley Refinery 4wPM Motor Rail

Manufacturer:	Motor Rail Ltd, Simplex Works, Bedford
Built:	No known
Works number:	Not known
Running numbers:	H11 (AGWI)
Engine:	20hp
Gauge:	2ft 0in
At Fawley:	1928 – 1948

Another of the 1928 Fawley arrivals about which little is known. This one survived the Second World War before being disposed of in 1948.

Fawley Refinery 4wPM Motor Rail No 1252

Manufacturer:	Motor Rail Ltd, Simplex Works, Bedford
Built:	1918
Works number:	1252
Running numbers:	H13, N.L.1 (both AGWI), D207 (Esso)
Engine:	20hp Dorman 2JO
Driving wheels:	1ft 6in
Wheelbase:	3ft 8in
Weight:	2ton 10cwt
Gauge:	2ft 0in
At Fawley:	1933 – 1957

Motor Rail No 1252 was supplied new to the War Department Light Railways in France in January 1918 and was one of the makers "Bent Frame" design. After leaving the military in 1919 it saw unrecorded civilian service and came to Fawley from Motor Rail by way of agent William Jones in February 1933. Its time at the refinery ended when sold to the Tottenham Imperial Works of Chessums Ltd in 1957 and nothing further is known.

Fawley Refinery 4wPM Motor Rail No 3896

Manufacturer:	Motor Rail Ltd, Simplex Works, Bedford
Built:	Rebuilt 1935 (from a 1928 model)
Works number:	3896 (previous number not known)
Running numbers:	H14 (AGWI)
Engine:	40hp Dorman 4JO
Wheelbase:	4ft 0in
Weight:	8ton 0cwt
At Fawley:	1935 – 1957

This loco was a rebuild of an earlier model, possibly dating from 1928 but its origin is not clear. However, it arrived at Fawley via agent William Jones in 1935. Its spell there lasted until it passed to dealers G.W. Bungey of Heston, Middlesex in June 1957 before being transferred to the Esso Tank farm at Purfleet, Essex and used at Harrison's Wharf Bitumen Terminal, where it was finally scrapped in 1967.

Fawley Refinery 4wPM Motor Rail No 4702

Manufacturer:	Motor Rail Ltd, Simplex Works, Bedford
Built:	1934
Works number:	4702
Running numbers:	H15, N.L.4 (Both AGWI)
Engine:	20/26hp Dorman 2JOR
Weight:	2ton 10cwt
Gauge:	2ft 0in
At Fawley:	1937 – 1957

No 4702 was supplied new to the firm of Petrol Loco Hirers Ltd (a subsidiary of Motor Rail) in November 1934 and purchased second hand by AGWI from Motor Rail themselves in October 1937. At some time in its Fawley career it exchanged identities with H.17 (Motor Rail No 4724) by way of the engine casings being swapped over. This loco was sold (together with No 3896) to dealer G.W. Bungey at Heston Airport, Middlesex in 1957 and nothing further is known.

Motor Rail No 1252/1918 on duty at Fawley with a train of asphalt drums, circa 1950. (Esso Petroleum Co)

Under wraps is the diminutive Motor Rail No 3896 photographed on 3rd June 1950.
(John A. Bailey/Bert Moody collection)

Fawley Refinery 4wPM Motor Rail No 4716

Manufacturer:	Motor Rail Ltd, Simplex Works, Bedford
Built:	1936
Works number:	4716
Running numbers:	H16, N.L.5 (Both AGWI)
Engine:	20/26hp Dorman 2JOR
Weight:	2ton 10cwt
Gauge:	2ft 0in
At Fawley:	1938 – 1957

No 4716 was another Motor Rail loco dispatched new to their subsidiary firm of Petrol Loco Hirers Ltd in December 1936 and afterwards delivered second hand by Motor Rail to AGWI in March 1938. Its time at Fawley refinery lasted until it was sold to the Lytchett Brick Co Ltd, Upton Brickworks, near Poole in 1957, after which it was disposed of around 1966.

Fawley Refinery 4wPM Motor Rail No 4724

Manufacturer:	Motor Rail Ltd, Simplex Works, Bedford
Built:	1939
Works number:	4724
Running numbers:	H17, N.L.2 (Both AGWI)
Engine:	20/26hp Dorman 2JOR
Weight:	2ton 10cwt
Gauge:	2ft 0in
At Fawley:	1939 – 1961

This was the final narrow gauge Motor Rail loco purchased by AGWI for use at their Fawley Refinery, arriving new from the makers in April 1939. As indicated in the notes for Motor Rail No 4702 the identities of the two locos were transposed when the engine casings were exchanged sometime during routine maintenance. As well as being the last arrival, this was also the last of the narrow gauge fleet to leave Esso. Its final duties involved the dismantling what remained of the refinery's narrow gauge system, after which it was donated to the Hampshire Narrow Gauge Railway Society at Stoke Park, Bishopstoke, Hampshire, in November 1961. There it was given the name "AGWI PET" in recognition of its previous owners, and also afforded the luxury of an enclosed cab – built from remnants of main line steam locos broken up at the nearby Eastleigh BR works. The Society moved to Durley in 1968 but the site was abandoned in 1992. Now, under the ownership of The Hampshire Narrow Gauge Railway Trust, the loco is housed at Bursledon Brickworks where it regularly operates on the demonstration track.

Fawley Refinery 4wDM Motor Rail No 5755

Manufacturer:	Motor Rail Ltd, Simplex Works, Bedford
Built:	1948
Works number:	5755
Engine:	65/85hp Dorman 4DL
Weight:	15t 0cwt
At Fawley:	1949 – 1960

No 5755 was the last of three standard gauge Motor Rail locos to arrive at Fawley, having been delivered new from the makers in January 1949. Its time at the refinery lasted until 1960 when it was transferred to Esso's Purfleet Tank Farm and used at Harrison's Wharf Bitumen Terminal from 1964. Its final move was to Thomas W. Ward's Columbia Wharf at Grays where it was scrapped in 1967.

Loco No H16 (Motor Rail No 4716) captured in an off duty moment on 3rd June 1950.
(John A. Bailey/Bert Moody collection)

No H17 (Motor Rail No 4724) or is it really H15? (see the notes on these locos) pictured at Fawley on 3rd June 1950.
(John A. Bailey/Bert Moody collection)

The contrasting designs of Motor Rail locos are illustrated here on 3rd June 1950 with No 5755 nearest camera and No 4169 beyond.
(John A. Bailey/Bert Moody collection)

Fawley Refinery 0-4-4-0DE General Electric No 30483

Manufacturer:	General Electric Co, Erie, Pennsylvania, USA
Built:	1949
Works number:	30483
Running numbers:	124
Weight:	45ton 0cwt
At Fawley:	1950 – 1978

This powerful loco was sent over from America to assist in the rebuilding of Fawley Refinery, arriving from New York aboard the vessel *Vandalia* at Southampton Docks on 3rd January 1950 and was initially engaged in the building of a new branch line into the refinery from the exchange sidings with BR's main line. It was afterwards employed in general duties until being retired in April 1978, and then was taken into preservation at the Steamtown Museum, Carnforth. Unfortunately, after many years of inactivity, plans for its restoration were abandoned and the loco was sent for scrap to the firm of C.F. Booth in May 2005, being broken up later that year.

Fawley Refinery 4wDH Hibberd No 3454

Manufacturer:	F.C. Hibberd & Co Ltd, Park Royal, London
Built:	1950
Works number:	3454
Engine:	Lister 27/3
Weight:	4ton 10cwt
Gauge:	3ft 0in
At Fawley:	1950 – 1951

This "Planet" locomotive was one of an initial pair (the other being 3467) that were delivered to Danish contractors Christiani & Nielsen Ltd during the works for building new jetties when the refinery was expanded and rebuilt during 1950/1. It arrived new in March 1950 and was one of several supplied to the Fawley site. There is a possibility that this loco was one of a pair that was later used during the construction of Southampton's Northam Bridge in 1952/3 but nothing further is recorded after this contract ended.

Fawley Refinery 4wDH Hibberd No 3467

Manufacturer:	F.C. Hibberd & Co Ltd, Park Royal, London
Built:	1950
Works number:	3467
Engine:	Lister 27/3
Weight:	4ton 10cwt
Gauge:	3ft 0in
At Fawley:	1950 – 1951

This "Planet" locomotive arrived in March 1950, together with No 3454, being the first pair of several such locos supplied new to Danish contractors Christiani & Nielsen Ltd for building the new refinery jetties during 1950/1. It is possible that this loco and its sister also worked on C&N's contract for the construction of Southampton's Northam Bridge in 1952/3 but nothing further is known.

A Yank at Fawley - General Electric 0-4-4-0DE No 30483 in Esso livery on 1st April 1962.
(Roger Holmes)

One of several 3ft gauge "Planet" type contractor's locos employed during the expansion of the refinery. This was either No 3454 or 3467 which were the only two on site when this photograph was taken on the 3rd June 1950.
(John A. Bailey/Bert Moody Collection)

Fawley Refinery 4wDH Hibberd No 3468

Manufacturer:	F.C. Hibberd & Co Ltd, Park Royal, London
Built:	1950
Works number:	3468
Engine:	Lister 27/3
Weight:	4ton 10cwt
Gauge:	3ft 0in
At Fawley:	1950 – 1951

Hibberd No 3468 was the third 3ft gauge loco supplied to Danish contractors Christiani & Nielsen Ltd, arriving new at Fawley in July 1950, where works for the huge expansion of the refinery took almost two years to complete. After working at Fawley, it was next recorded with the Cementation Company Ltd at Bentley Works, Doncaster, being afterwards dispatched to the Rufford Colliery, Mansfield in December 1952. This was its last reported move.

Fawley Refinery 4wDH Hibberd No 3472

Manufacturer:	F.C. Hibberd & Co Ltd, Park Royal, London
Built:	1950
Works number:	3472
Engine:	Lister 27/3
Weight:	4ton 10cwt
Gauge:	3ft 0in
At Fawley:	1950 – 1951

Hibberd No 3472 was the fourth 3ft gauge Planet loco supplied to Danish contractors Christiani & Nielsen Ltd, arriving new at Fawley in November 1950. Like its sister engine No 3468, its was next recorded with the Cementation Company Ltd at Bentley Works, Doncaster, before being dispatched to the Rufford Colliery, Mansfield in December 1952. This was also its last reported move.

Fawley Refinery 4wDH Hibberd No 3496

Manufacturer:	F.C. Hibberd & Co Ltd, Park Royal, London
Built:	1950
Works number:	3496
Engine:	Lister 18/2
Weight:	4ton 10cwt
Gauge:	3ft 0in
At Fawley:	1950 – 1951

There is an element of doubt as to whether this loco actually worked at Fawley where it was scheduled for dispatch to contractors Christiani & Nielsen in November 1950 along with sister No 3472. However, the maker's works list shows the same job number repeated almost two years later when it was sent to the firm of Henckell Du Buisson & Co in St Lucia in July 1952 for work on their West Indian sugar plantations, after which no further record is known.

Fawley Refinery 0-4-0DH North British No 27078

Manufacturer:	North British Locomotive Co Ltd, Glasgow
Built:	1953
Works number:	27078
Running numbers:	2058
Engine:	200hp Paxman 6RPH
Driving wheels:	3ft 6in
Wheelbase:	6ft 0in
Weight:	32ton 0cwt
At Fawley:	1953 – 1980

This North British demonstration loco was sold to Esso and arrived at Fawley in 1953. There it was engaged in general duties until moving into preservation at the Mid-Hants Railway in November 1980, but its short lived retirement ended when it was scrapped in July 1986.

Fawley Refinery 0-4-0DH North British No 27415

Manufacturer:	North British Locomotive Co Ltd, Glasgow
Built:	1954
Works number:	27415
Running numbers:	2059
Engine:	300hp Paxman 6RPHX
Driving wheels:	3ft 6in
Wheelbase:	6ft 0in
Weight:	32ton 0cwt
At Fawley:	1955 – 1980

This was the second of two North British locos at Fawley and, like the other one, it was a demonstration loco before being purchased. One of its first appearances was at the West India Docks in London in July 1954 and by September that year it was showing its paces at Willesden. A month later it had moved to Southampton Docks where it was on trial for three months, after which it was bought by Esso and taken to Fawley in January 1955. Its duties at the refinery lasted until 1980 when it was presented to the Wight Locomotive Society for preservation. The loco was afterwards transferred to the Scottish Railway Preservation Society at Bo'ness in 1991 where it still resides and carries the name *Tiger*.

North British loco No 27415 pictured in Southampton's Eastern Docks on 3rd December 1954 where it was on trial for three months.
(Associated British Ports)

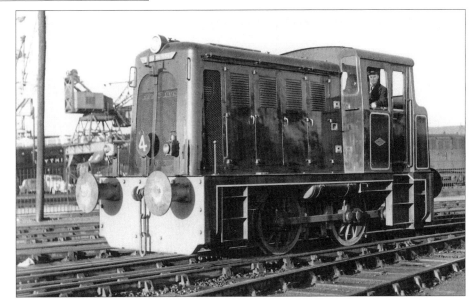

North British loco No 27078 bids goodbye to Fawley in November 1980, destined for a brief retirement.
(Dave Blay)

Fawley Refinery 0-4-0DH English Electric No 8423

Manufacturer:	English Electric Co Ltd, Stephenson Works, Darlington.
Built:	1963
Works number:	8423
Running numbers:	2339
Engine:	350hp Dorman 8QVA
Driving wheels:	3ft 4in
Wheelbase:	9ft 0in
Weight:	48ton 0cwt
At Fawley:	1963 – 1989

Arriving new from the makers in 1963, English Electric No 8423 laboured at Fawley refinery until sent for overhaul by Thomas Hill at Kilnhurst in June 1981, returning to Fawley in April the following year. In 1989 it was sold to D.S. Procurements Ltd, Hythe, remaining there until sent for scrap to Booth-Rowe Metals Ltd, Rotherham, in January 1991.

Fawley Refinery 4wDH Rolls Royce No 10197

Manufacturer:	Rolls Royce Ltd, Sentinel Works, Shrewsbury
Built:	1965
Works number:	10197
Running numbers:	2034
Engine:	255hp R-R C6SFL
Driving wheels:	3ft 2in
Wheelbase:	6ft 6in
Weight:	34ton 0cwt
At Fawley:	1976 – 1983

Rolls Royce No 10197 came off the assembly line in October 1964 and was delivered new to Esso at their Salt End, Hull refinery in 1965. In 1976 it was transferred to Fawley where it remained until June 1983 when sold to Resco (Railways) Ltd, at Erith in Kent before moving to Thomas Hill at Kilnhurst, Yorkshire for overhaul. After this, it went to the Blue Circle Industries cement works at Weardale, Co Durham in September 1984. The works were later taken over by Lafarge Cement and the loco is currently stored there out of use

Fawley Refinery 0-6-0DH Hunslet/Andrew Barclay No 7542

Name:	*Greenfinch*
Manufacturer:	Hunslet Engine Co Ltd, Hunslet, Leeds
Built:	1978
Works number:	648 (Andrew Barclay), renumbered as Hunslet No 7542
Running numbers:	553
Engine:	420hp G-Motors 12V71N
Driving wheels:	3ft 9in
Wheelbase:	9ft 6in
Weight:	45ton 0cwt
At Fawley:	1978 – 2003

Having arrived new at Fawley in 1978, this Hunslet loco was originally constructed as Andrew Barclay & Sons No 648 (Barclays being taken over by Hunslet and a new number allocated before leaving the works). Its work at the refinery ended when it was dismantled there and stripped for spares in December 2003. However, its main motor remains in use elsewhere on a maritime oil platform.

A glimpse of English Electric No 843/1963 on the main sidings at Fawley Refinery. (Dave Blay)

Rolls Royce No 10197/1965 in its Fawley days. (Dave Blay)

"Greenfinch" pictured on the refinery main line shortly before disposal. (Dave Blay)

Fawley Refinery 0-6-0DH Hunslet No 8999

Name:	*Redwing*
Manufacturer:	Hunslet Engine Co Ltd, Hunslet, Leeds
Built:	1981
Works number:	8999
Running numbers:	641
Engine:	420hp G-Motors 12V71N
Driving wheels:	3ft 9in
Wheelbase:	9ft 6in
Weight:	45ton 0cwt
At Fawley:	1981 – 2004 and 2007 – present day

Having arrived new in 1981 and having given over two decades of service, this Hunslet loco went back to its makers and was sent for overhaul by the LH Group at Barton-under-Needwood in April 2004. Further work was carried out at the Statfold Barn Railway in Staffordshire from December 2006 before the loco was returned to Fawley in August 2007.

Fawley Refinery 0-6-0DH Hunslet No 8998

Name:	*Bluebird*
Manufacturer:	Hunslet Engine Co Ltd, Hunslet, Leeds
Built:	1981
Works number:	8998
Running numbers:	552
Engine:	420hp G-Motors 12V71N
Driving wheels:	3ft 9in
Wheelbase:	9ft 6in
Weight:	45ton 0cwt
At Fawley:	1985 – 2007 and 2008 – present day

Supplied new to Esso at their Milford Haven, Dyfed refinery in February 1981, this loco moved to Fawley in July 1985. In August 2007 it was sent back to the makers for overhaul at the Statfold Barn Railway in Staffordshire and returned to Fawley in April 2008.

Fawley Refinery 4wDH Thomas Hill No 285V

Manufacturer:	Thomas Hill (Rotherham) Ltd, Kilnhurst, Yorks
Built:	1979
Works number:	285V
Engine:	300hp Rolls-Royce C6TFL
Driving wheels:	3ft 6in
Wheelbase:	9ft 0in
Weight:	35ton 0cwt
At Fawley:	1999

This Thomas Hill Vanguard loco was delivered new in 1979 to Rowntree Macintosh at their York factory and remained there until the works rail system declined. It was then acquired by Hunslet Barclay by September 1990 and, after a rebuild by them, worked on hire to ICI at their Billingham works in 1993/4, before returning to Barclay's at Kilmarnock. There next came a spell at Ford's plant in Bridgend in February 1998 and by spring 1999 it had arrived on hire for six months duty at Fawley refinery. By November 2000 it had been sold to the Lindsey Oil Refinery at Killingholme in Lincolnshire where it is still currently employed carrying the name *Tigger*.

Hunslet No 8999/1981 rests between duties at Fawley on 15th April 2008. (Author)

HE No 8998 "Bluebird" marshals a train on the Fawley main line. (Dave Blay)

Thomas Hill No 285V sporting a Barclay plate and ICI logo while on duty at Fawley in 1999. (Dave Blay)

Fawley Refinery 0-6-0DH Andrew Barclay No 659

Name:	*Sam (Gillian)*
Manufacturer:	Andrew Barclay Ltd, Caledonia Works, Kilmarnock
Built:	1982
Works number:	659* (Rebuilt as Hunslet/Andrew Barclay 6769 in 1990)
Running numbers:	MSC2
Engine:	420hp G-Motors 12V71N
Driving wheels:	3ft 9in
Wheelbase:	9ft 6in
Weight:	45ton 0cwt
At Fawley:	2006 – 2008

This loco was originally built as Andrew Barclay No 659 of 1982 vintage when supplied new to the National Coal Board at Seaham, Co Durham. In 1988 it was sent to Hunslet/Barclay (the manufacturer's successors) for a rebuild, re-emerging as their No 6769 some two years later and employed by Corus at their Ebbw Vale steelworks from about the end of 1990 where it carried the name *Gillian*. It left there in January 2004 and by March that year it was with the LH Group, Barton-under-Needwood, where it underwent another rebuild. It appeared at the Manchester Ship Canal (via trials on the Foxfield Railway) some three months later, running there as MSC2 and carrying the name *Sam*. After that it was again at the LHG for repairs from April 2005 before transfer to the St. Gobain Pipeworks at their Stanton Works in Derbyshire in June that year. Following yet another visit the LHG in February 2006 it travelled to Fawley that April as a replacement for HE No 8999 and, afterwards, HE No 8998 until departing in April 2008.

*Due to an error it emerged from its 2004 rebuild carrying the Barclay works plate of No 660 which it carried until the correct plate No 659 was fixed by Hunslet at Fawley in 2007.

Hunslet/Andrew Barclay No 6769 carried the name "Gillian" at Ebbw Vale and is pictured there on 29th March 1996 having been rebuilt by Hunslet/Barclay in 1990. (Andy Williams)

Fawley Power Station 1964 – 1978

Fawley Power Station was built by the Central Electricity Generating Board in the 1960s and stands on the shore of Ower Lake, just to the north of Calshot, at the entrance to Southampton Water. Work began in 1964 and contractors Taylor Woodrow Plant Co Ltd employed eight narrow gauge battery electric locomotives during the construction works, which lasted for three years. The locos were all built by Wingrove & Rogers Ltd, of Kirkby, Liverpool, six of which arrived new, with two others being transferred from other contracts. At the same time, a 10ft diameter tunnel, approximately two miles long, was built under Southampton water to carry national grid high voltage cables from the power station to the opposite shore at Chilling, and a narrow gauge railway was laid through this to assist in maintenance of the cables. This was operated by a small Greenwood and Batley loco propelling trolleys through the tunnel.

When the power station was completed in 1967 most of the WR locos were transferred to the contractor's depot at Greenford, Middlesex where some were scrapped soon after arrival, but others were subsequently employed on other projects. The tunnel system, also completed in 1967, remained active until the underground loco was scrapped in 1978, although the trolleys have occasionally been hand propelled since then. The power station is oil fired, taking supply from a pipeline connection to the adjacent refinery, and is currently operating at half capacity, coming on line only when demand is greatest.

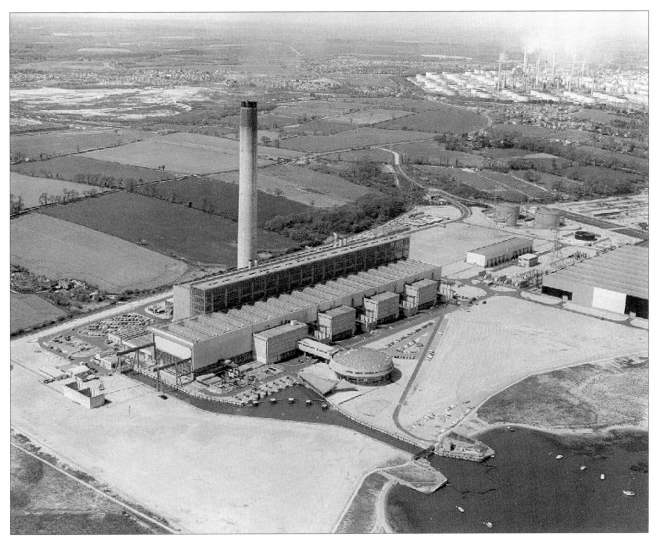

An aerial view of Fawley Power Station with the refinery in the top right of the photo. (Author's Collection)

Fawley Power Station 4wBE Wingrove & Rogers No D6776

Manufacturer:	Wingrove & Rogers Ltd, Kirkby, Liverpool
Built:	1964
Works number:	D6776
Gauge:	2ft 0in
At Fawley:	1964 – 1967

This loco was one of six delivered new to the contractors, Taylor Woodrow, for construction of the Fawley Power Station in 1964. After the project was completed, it was scrapped at Taylor Woodrow's depot in Greenford, Middlesex.

Fawley Power Station 4wBE Wingrove & Rogers No D6864

Manufacturer:	Wingrove & Rogers Ltd, Kirkby, Liverpool
Built:	1964
Works number:	D6864
Gauge:	2ft 0in
At Fawley:	1964 – 1967

The second of six Wingrove & Rogers locos delivered new to the contractors Taylor Woodrow for construction of the Fawley Power Station in 1964. When the work was completed it was taken to Taylor Woodrow's depot in Greenford, Middlesex where it was subsequently scrapped by 1975.

Fawley Power Station 4wBE Wingrove & Rogers No D6865

Manufacturer:	Wingrove & Rogers Ltd, Kirkby, Liverpool
Built:	1964
Works number:	D6865
Gauge:	2ft 0in
At Fawley:	1964 – 1967

Another of the six Wingrove & Rogers locos used by contractors Taylor Woodrow for construction of the Fawley Power Station. Having been delivered new in 1964, it was taken to Taylor Woodrow's Greenford, Middlesex Depot after the project was completed and was subsequently scrapped there by 1975.

Fawley Power Station 4wBE Wingrove & Rogers No D6868

Manufacturer:	Wingrove & Rogers Ltd, Kirkby, Liverpool
Built:	1964
Works number:	D6868
Gauge:	2ft 0in
At Fawley:	1964 – 1967

One of the six Wingrove & Rogers locos used by contractors Taylor Woodrow in the construction of the Fawley Power Station, where it was delivered new in 1964. When work was complete it was taken to the owner's depot at Greenford, Middlesex where it was subsequently scrapped by 1975.

Fawley Power Station 4wBE Wingrove & Rogers No D6869

Manufacturer:	Wingrove & Rogers Ltd, Kirkby, Liverpool
Built:	1964
Works number:	D6869
Gauge:	2ft 0in
At Fawley:	1964 – 1967

This Wingrove & Rogers loco was one of six WR locos supplied new to contractors Taylor Woodrow in 1964 for the construction of the Fawley Power Station. After the project was completed it was last recorded at Taylor Woodrow's depot in Greenford, Middlesex where it was scrapped by 1975.

Fawley Power Station 4wBE Wingrove & Rogers No D6904

Manufacturer:	Wingrove & Rogers Ltd, Kirkby, Liverpool
Built:	1964
Works number:	D6904
Gauge:	2ft 0in
At Fawley:	1964 – 1967

One of a batch of six W&R locos supplied new to contractors Taylor Woodrow for the construction of Fawley Power Station. When work was completed in 1967 it is thought to have been used on other projects before eventually being scrapped at Taylor Woodrow's depot in Greenford, Middlesex.

Fawley Power Station 0-4-0BE Wingrove & Rogers No 5933

Manufacturer:	Wingrove & Rogers Ltd, Kirkby, Liverpool
Built:	1958
Works number:	5933
Gauge:	2ft 0in
At Fawley:	1965 – 1967

This was one of a pair of older Wingrove & Rogers locos used by Taylor Woodrow in the construction of Fawley Power Station, arriving on the scene from another CEGB project at Hinkley Point, Somerset in July 1965, a little later than the new locos which were supplied a year earlier. After the works were complete in 1967 it was transferred to the owners Greenford Depot in Middlesex where it was scrapped in November 1968.

Fawley Power Station 0-4-0BE Wingrove & Rogers No 6127

Manufacturer:	Wingrove & Rogers Ltd, Kirkby, Liverpool
Built:	1958
Works number:	6127
Gauge:	2ft 0in
At Fawley:	1965 – 1967

This was the second loco of a pair of 1958 Wingrove & Rogers locos to arrive at Fawley in July 1965 from Taylor Woodrow's earlier CEGB contract at Hinkley Point in Somerset. However, unlike the sister engine (No 5933) it accompanied, it is thought to have been scrapped upon completion of the Fawley project in 1967.

Fawley Power Station 4wBE Greenwood & Batley No 420060

Manufacturer:	Greenwood & Batley Ltd, Leeds
Built:	1967
Works number:	420060
Engine:	2hp
Wheelbase:	3ft 6in
Weight:	2ton 13.5cwt
Gauge:	3ft 1⅛in
At Fawley:	1967 – 1978

This specialised locomotive was delivered new to contractors Taylor Woodrow on site in July 1967 for maintenance use in the 10ft diameter tunnel that carried high voltage cables under Southampton Water. It had a top speed of 6mph and could haul loads of up to 10ton. Salt water was pumped through the tunnel to cool the cables and the damp, corrosive conditions finally took their toll on the loco when, after little more than a decade, it was considered no longer safe to use. There being no way to bring it to the surface, it was scrapped underground in 1978.

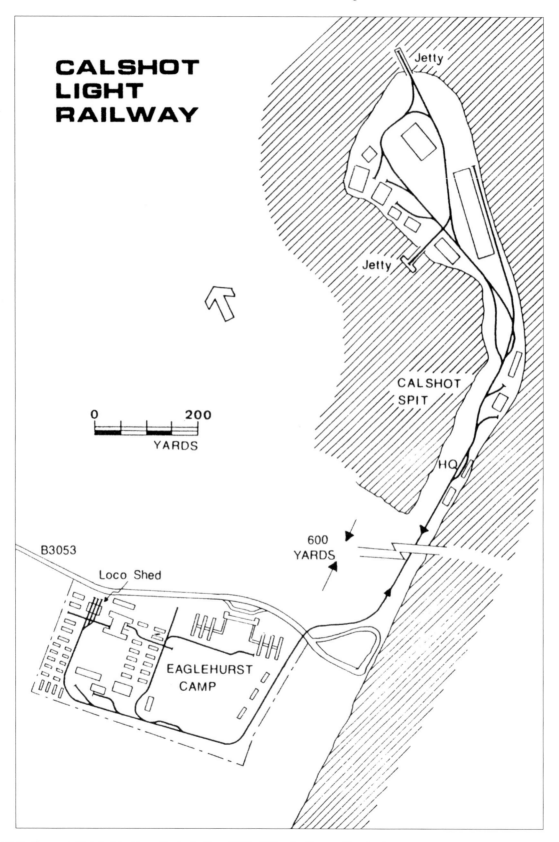

CALSHOT
LIGHT
RAILWAY

Jetty

Jetty

CALSHOT
SPIT

HQ

600
YARDS

B3053

Loco Shed

EAGLEHURST
CAMP

0   200
YARDS

The RAF Railway at Calshot in its entirety, before 1921. (Map by Roger Hateley)

CHAPTER 15

Calshot Railway 1913 – 1949

The remote spit of land at Calshot was chosen by the Admiralty as one of many sites around the coast of Britain for a series of air stations that would defend the realm in times of warfare. Having been built by March 1913 it was soon employed in the operation of seaplanes for the protection of shipping during the First World War.

The base was considerably expanded in 1916, the works being carried out by contractor Henry Boot & Son (Westminster) Ltd who used one locomotive (and possibly a second) that had previously been employed on a nearby gravel pit (also owned by Boot), and then engaged during the construction of the camp. The locos he used there were 0-4-0 well tanks, built by Hudswell Clarke.

Eaglehurst Camp was established just under a mile inland from the original air station. The former 2ft 0in gauge construction railway was expanded to serve the whole length of the complex, from the camp to the jetty at the seaward end, and was operated by Boot & Son until 1919 when the line was taken over by the RAF (which came into being in April 1918). Its complete length was 1 mile and 52 chains with a three-road loco shed at the camp terminus.

Apart from conveying goods and stores, the railway (affectionately known as the *Calshot Express*) also operated a passenger timetable for service personnel who were carried from the camp to the Spit in four-wheel wagons that had roofs for shelter but open sides. There were, however, two enclosed wagons for officers.

Towards the end of 1918 two Baguley 0-4-0 petrol locos arrived at Calshot during construction works for the RAF camp, but these were never highly regarded and both had been disposed of within two years. Following their departure, a Kerr, Stuart "Wren" Class 0-4-0ST (No 4019/1918) arrived in 1920, having previously worked at Totton while engaged in forestry work. This was followed in late 1921 by two Barclay 0-4-0WT locos, these being numbers 1431 and 1453, both having been built in 1918.

The Kerr, Stuart loco was soon discarded, and by 1923 had been sold to dealers Wm. Jones of Greenwich, whilst the Barclay duo continued to operate the camp service until 1931, when No 1453 was exchanged for No 1432, a sister engine in storage at the Air Ministry's West Drayton depot.

No further changes to the motive power occurred before the line ceased operation at the end of World War Two. By then the equipment and rolling stock were in poor condition and taken out of use, with the locos being stored in the running shed for some years while the track was gradually dismantled and the various artefacts sold off for scrap. The final disposals were the locomotives themselves, both being dispatched to Abelson & Co of Birmingham in April 1949.

The RAF closed Eaglehurst Camp in May 1961 and there is now little evidence of it or its railway. The Officers' Mess became the "Owl & Crescent" public house, which was later renamed "The Flying Boat". However, due to lack of trade it closed in the late 1990s and, after falling into a derelict state, was destroyed by fire in July 2001. At the Spit end, several of the hangars and sheds remain today as part of the Calshot Activities Centre.

A snowy scene at the new Calshot Naval Air Station in 1913. Many buildings are established and two small seaplanes (one wingless) stand near the slipway at the centre left of the picture.
(Author's Collection)

Rush hour on the "Calshot Express". This posed photograph from July 1920 shows a little overcrowding on the train to Eaglehurst Camp, but the airmen seem happy enough. (Author's Collection)

One of the Andrew Barclay 0-4-0WTs with a train approaching Calshot Spit in 1929. (Author's Collection)

The "Calshot Express" crosses the Calshot roadway on its way to Eaglehurst Camp. (Edward Mudge postcard)

Another Mudge study shows one of the Barclay locomotives with a train at the Spit camp gates heading for Eaglehurst. (Edward Mudge postcard)

Calshot Railway 0-4-0WT Hudswell Clarke No 1129

Manufacturer:	Hudswell Clarke & Co Ltd, Leeds
Built:	1915
Works number:	1129
Cylinders:	5ins x 8ins
Driving wheels:	1ft 8ins
Weight:	4ton 13cwt
Gauge:	2ft 0in
At Calshot:	1916 – 1919

Having been built in May 1915 No 1129 was delivered new to contractor W. Alban Richards & Co at Abergele, North Wales, for use during the construction of Kimmel Park Army Camp near St. Asaph. Work there finished in August 1916 and by the following month it is thought No 1129 had found its way to Calshot. Henry Boot & Son (Westminster) Ltd is presumed to have employed the loco (and at least one other) at his gravel pit during the construction of Eaglehurst Camp. It was then subsequently engaged during his operation of the railway between the camp and the Air Ministry station at Calshot Spit, until the line was taken over by the RAF who engaged replacement locomotives in 1919. This engine was then possibly relocated to another Boot contract but no further record of its later employment is known.

Calshot Railway 0-4-0PM Baguley Cars No 756

Manufacturer:	Baguley Cars Ltd, Burton-upon-Trent, Staffordshire
Built:	1918
Works number:	756
Engine:	10hp
Driving wheels:	1ft 6in
Wheelbase:	2ft 6in
Weight:	1ton 5cwt
Gauge:	2ft 0in
At Calshot:	1918 – 1919

Baguley No 756 was one of a pair of petrol locos that had a short and unsuccessful spell operating on the Calshot Light Railway during construction of the RAF camp. This model arrived new from the makers in November 1918 but was soon dispensed with in the following year, and no further records exist; its sister, No 757 lasted a little longer.

Calshot Railway 0-4-0PM Baguley Cars No 757

Manufacturer:	Baguley Cars Ltd, Burton-upon-Trent, Staffordshire
Built:	1918
Works number:	757
Engine:	10hp
Driving wheels:	1ft 6in
Wheelbase:	2ft 6in
Weight:	1ton 5cwt
Gauge:	2ft 0in
At Calshot:	1918 – 1920

One of a pair of Baguley petrol locos deployed without success during construction of the RAF camp. Having arrived new from the makers in December 1918, this one lasted a little longer than its sister and was next recorded under the ownership of A. Robertson Ltd, in October 1920. Nothing further is known.

Calshot Railway 0-4-0ST Kerr, Stuart No 4019

Manufacturer:	Kerr, Stuart & Co Ltd, California Works, Stoke on Trent
Built:	1919
Works number:	4019
Cylinders:	6ins x 9ins
Driving wheels:	1ft 8ins
Wheelbase:	3ft 0in
Working pressure:	140psi
Water capacity:	87gals
Weight:	4ton 13cwt
Gauge:	2ft 0in
At Calshot:	1920 – 1921

This "Wren" class loco was one of a consignment ordered for the Ministry of Munitions factory at Renfrew, Scotland, but by the time it had been dispatched in February 1919 it is thought that the destination had been amended to the Board of Trade's Timber Supply Department's premises in Totton, Hampshire. Whatever the reality, it was already at Calshot when two Barclay locos arrived in late 1921. However, its time there was short, as it would seem that the arrival of the Barclays prompted its sale to dealer Wm. Jones of Greenwich, and an onward dispatch to the Ham River Grit Company's gravel pits near Kingston in London around 1923/4. Spares for this loco were dispatched to Ham at Twickenham and it was next noted being overhauled by Kerr Stuart in May 1925 before going to contractors Aubrey Watson Ltd who are thought to have used this loco on their construction of the Wansford by-pass near Peterborough in 1928/9. Its next appearance was at the East Midland Gravel Company's Wansford pits in February 1930, but by 1939 it had disappeared and is assumed to have been scrapped by then.

Calshot Railway 0-4-0WT Andrew Barclay No 1431

Manufacturer:	Andrew Barclay Sons & Co Ltd, Caledonia Works, Kilmarnock
Built:	1918
Works number:	1431
Cylinders:	6¾ins x 10¾ins
Driving wheels:	1ft 10ins
Wheelbase:	3ft 11¼in
Working pressure:	160psi
Water capacity:	120 gals
Weight:	6ton 15cwt
Gauge:	2ft 0in
At Calshot:	1921 – 1949

Andrew Barclay No 1431 was delivered ex works in February 1918 to the Admiralty Air Construction Corps at Hanworth Road Siding, Sunbury, and was employed by them at Manston, Kent during that year. By October 1921 it had arrived at Calshot where it was joined a month later by sister engine No 1453. Its active life at Eaglehurst lasted until the end of WWII when the line fell out of use and the locos were placed in store until 1949. It was sold by auctioneers Henry Butcher & Co in April that year, and purchased by the engineering firm of Abelson & Co of Birmingham for £60. There it was given a complete overhaul and presented to the Talyllyn Railway in April 1953 where it was converted to a gauge of 2ft 3in. On the Talyllyn Railway it carries the name *Douglas* after one of Abelson's directors, and is still in regular service.

See page 122 for an illustration of this locomotive

Andrew Barclay No 1431 as "Douglas" in preservation on the Talyllyn Railway in September 1969. (Author)

Andrew Barclay No 1453 pictured in its final days at Walston's Alston Lime Company. (Frank Jones Collection/IRS)

Barclay No1432/1918 stands with a train at the camp on Calshot Spit in pre-WWII days. (R.D. Darvill collection)

Calshot Railway 0-4-0WT Andrew Barclay No 1453

Manufacturer:	Andrew Barclay Sons & Co Ltd, Caledonia Works, Kilmarnock
Built:	1918
Works number:	1453
Cylinders:	6¾in x 10¾in
Driving wheels:	1ft 10ins
Wheelbase:	3ft 11¼in
Working pressure:	160psi
Water capacity:	120 gals
Weight:	6ton 15cwt
Gauge:	2ft 0in
At Calshot:	1921 – 1931

As with its Calshot sisters, Barclay No 1453 first saw the light of day at the Admiralty Air Construction Corps at Hanworth Road Siding, Sunbury, having left the maker's works in April 1918. Its first assignment was at the Dymchurch Aerodrome later that year, before moving to Calshot in November 1921, where it joined No 1431. By 1931, heavy repairs were needed and this loco was sent to the Air Ministry depot at West Drayton where it was exchanged for No 1432. There it was auctioned by Fuller, Horsey & Co, along with seven other locos, in March that year, being purchased by the Durham County Water Board and employed in the construction of Burnhope Reservoir. That project lasted until 1938, after which it was sold to the nearby Walston's Alston Lime Co where it remained until being broken up sometime during the Second World War.

Calshot Railway 0-4-0WT Andrew Barclay No 1432

Manufacturer:	Andrew Barclay Sons & Co Ltd, Caledonia Works, Kilmarnock
Built:	1918
Works number:	1432
Cylinders:	6¾in x 10¾in
Driving wheels:	1ft 10ins
Wheelbase:	3ft 11¼in
Working pressure:	160psi
Water capacity:	120 gals
Weight:	6ton 15cwt
Gauge:	2ft 0in
At Calshot:	1931 – 1949

Andrew Barclay No 1432 left the maker's works in February 1918 and accompanied sister engine No 1431 to the Admiralty Air Construction Corps at Hanworth Road Siding, Sunbury, before moving onto the Ford Junction (Aerodrome) on the LB&SCR in its first year. After WWI hostilities ceased it was placed into store at the Air Ministry Transport Depot at West Drayton. There it remained unused until exchanged for Andrew Barclay No 1453 and sent to Calshot around 1931, serving its time along with No 1431 until the line ceased operation and, along with that loco, was sold by auction and purchased by Abelson & Co Birmingham in April 1949. Its stay at Abelson's engineering works ended when it was finally broken up March 1956.

CHAPTER 16

The Chapel Tramway 1843 – 1967

The Chapel Tramway had been constructed in 1843 by a Mr Pritchard for the purpose of linking the premises along the River Itchen Wharves to the main London to Southampton Railway at a junction to the north of Chapel Road. The line ran from its most northerly extent at Britannia Wharf, down along Marine Parade, then westwards through the gasworks and across Melbourne Street. However, it wasn't until as late as 1899 that steam traction took over from horses. The first locomotive being purchased by J.R Wood & Co in the form of a small Peckett engine No 438 built in 1884. This was followed by Barclay No 923 which was new in 1902 and another Peckett No 1375, also new in 1914. The original single road loco shed was at Burnley Wharf, alongside Marine Parade, near the overhead the coal conveyor that crossed the roadway. It appears in a 1924 photograph but a new two-road version was built at Victoria Wharf soon afterwards.

The final arrival, and last loco to work the line, was a second Barclay No 1398 of 1915 vintage, which was employed from 1961. Trade from the wharves had dwindled badly by the 1960s and closure of the system finally came in March 1967.

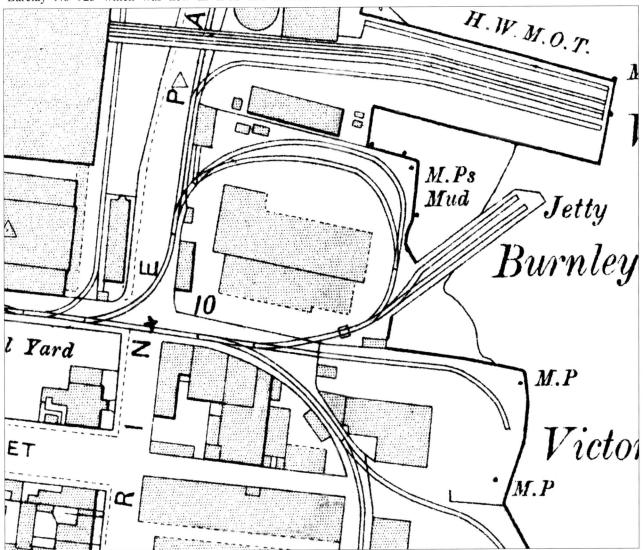

Above: This section of a 1910 Ordnance Survey map shows the position of original loco shed adjacent to Marine Parade on Burnley Wharf. (Reproduced from 1910 Ordnance Survey map with the kind permission of the Ordnance Survey.)

Left: This view of the Tramway from Victoria Wharf was taken on 8th May 1955 and looks westwards through the gasworks towards Melbourne Street. Marine Parade runs left to right across the picture and the line from the wharves joins at this point. (Roger Holmes)

The Chapel Tramway seen looking southwards along Marine Parade as Andrew Barclay No 1398 propels a train destined for Britannia Wharf in the line's final year of operation. (Bert Moody)

Almost the end of the line at Melbourne Street, quite literally as the road crossing on the right leads to the weed covered tracks approaching the gate to the main line exchange sidings. This desolate scene was observed on 11th June 1964. (Bert Moody)

The tramway's heyday is reflected in this photo of the railway's first Barclay No 923 rounding the curve at the Marine Parade crossing on 26th August 1948. (John A. Bailey/Bert Moody collection)

Peckett No 1375 was photographed at the same location on 8th May 1955. (Roger Holmes)

Above: This picture of the gasworks and Itchen wharves, with Marine Parade running diagonally across the middle, shows the Chapel Tramway in 1924. The original loco shed with Andrew Barclay No 923 is just visible to the right of the overhead conveyor gantry.
(KRM Collection)

Left: The Tramway's second Barclay No 1138 ventures out on to the main line exchange sidings and meets a BR counterpart in August 1966. (Roger Holmes)

Dibles Wharf 1869 – 1987

Over the years, the "Bull's Run" to Dibles Wharf had seen a succession of steam locomotives come and go. Former Southampton Dock Company 0-4-0ST *Bretwalda* arrived in 1926 and was followed by two Pecketts, the first being No 1638 of 1923 named *Bristol,* which appeared in 1935, followed by the unnamed No 2128, which arrived new from the makers in 1952. Both Pecketts were sold for scrap in 1963 and 1965 respectively and these were followed by ex-LSWR B4 class No 30096 *Corrall Queen* in 1963 and, finally, RSH No 7544 of 1949 *Bonnie Prince Charlie* in 1965.

In 1968 operators PD Fuels decided to switch to diesel power and 0-4-0DM Baguley No 3568 built in 1961 was purchased from brewers Bass, Mitchell & Butlers of Burton-upon-Trent in February of that year. It carried the logo *PD No 1* even though *Corrall Queen* and *Bonnie Prince Charlie* were still in residence. The pair were by now being regarded as merely back up engines – in fact

Bonnie Prince Charlie had never been employed much at all during its four year stay at Dibles. The two steamers were eventually taken into preservation in 1969 and 1972 respectively and *PD No 1* was joined by former Portsmouth Dockyard 0-4-0DM, a Hunslet, No 4262, built in 1952, which arrived on the wharf in January 1971, its naval identity being *Yard No 6952.*

The Hunslet lasted until July 1975, when it left for the nearby scrap merchants of Pollock, Brown & Co and was replaced by the biggest and most powerful of all the Dibles fleet. Hudswell Clarke D1253, an 0-6-0DM of 1962 vintage, arrived from the Manchester Ship Canal Co Ltd in December 1975 and became the final engine to trundle the rails at Dibles, forming a partnership with *PD No 1* until rail operations ceased there in 1987, the two locos being stored at the Haydon Bailey Private Museum on the adjacent James Wharf, before they were finally disposed of for scrap.

Dibles first Peckett "Bristol" leaves the gasworks cutting and heads across Britannia Road on 16th September 1953. (SUIAG)

Peckett No 2128 gets busy at Dibles Wharf on 1st April 1962. (Roger Holmes)

Steam days on the Bull's Run as B4 "Corrall Queen" heads through the cutting between Britannia and Belvidere Roads towards Dibles Wharf. (Bert Moody Collection)

Dibles Wharf 0-4-0DM Baguley No 3568

Manufacturer:	E.E. Baguley Ltd, Burton-upon-Trent, Staffs
Built:	1961
Works number:	3568
Running number:	No 1
Engine:	200hp Gardner 8L3
Driving Wheels:	3ft 6in
At Dibles Wharf:	1968 – 1987

Baguley No 3568 was built in May 1961 and delivered new to nearby brewers Bass, Mitchell & Butlers at Burton-upon-Trent, Staffordshire, where it was employed until being transferred to PD Fuels at Dibles Wharf in February 1968. Here it replaced the inadequate RSH 0-4-0ST *Bonnie Prince Charlie* and shared duties with the veteran B4 *Corrall Queen*, and also with successive diesel locos, remaining at the yard until rail operations ceased there in 1987, It was taken into storage at the Haydon Bailey Private Museum on the adjacent James Wharf, along with running mate Hudswell Clarke No D1253 where the pair suffered the same fate of being scrapped in March 1991.

Dibles Wharf 0-4-0DM Hunslet No 4262

Manufacturer:	Hunslet Engine Co Ltd, Hunslet, Leeds
Built:	1952
Works number:	4262
Running number:	Yard No 6952 (Navy)
Engine:	93/102hp Gardner 4L3
Driving Wheels:	3ft 4in
Wheelbase:	5ft 6in
Weight:	21ton 0cwt
At Dibles Wharf:	1971 – 1976

This Hunslet loco was delivered new to Portsmouth Dockyard in February 1952, its naval service lasting until January 1971 when sold to PD Fuels at Dibles Wharf. Its time there lasted until July 1976 when it moved the short distance up the River Itchen to its new owners, Pollock Brown & Co at Northam Iron Works (see Chapter 19) remaining there until scrapped in 1985.

Dibles Wharf 0-6-0DM Hudswell Clarke No D1253

Manufacturer:	Hunslet Engine Co Ltd, Hunslet, Leeds
Built:	1962
Works number:	D1253
Running number:	D9 (MSC)
Engine:	204hp Gardner 8L3
Driving Wheels:	3ft 4½in
Wheelbase:	8ft 7in
Weight:	36ton 0cwt
At Dibles Wharf:	1975 – 1987

Having been built in February 1962 and supplied new to the Manchester Ship Canal, this six coupled loco remained there until it moved to PD Fuels at Northam in December 1975, being the most powerful to operate at Dibles. After the end of rail operations there in 1987, it was stored at the Haydon Bailey Private Museum on the adjacent James Wharf, but was eventually scrapped in March 1991.

Baguley No 3568 was the first of a trio of diesels to operate at Dibles Wharf and is pictured there in June 1987.
(Bert Moody Collection)

Hudswell Clarke No D1253 at rest on in the final days of railway operation at Dibles Wharf in June 1987.
(Bert Moody Collection)

Hudswell Clarke No D1253/1962 seen crossing Britannia Road with a train of hopper wagons in July 1985.
(Bert Moody Collection)

CHAPTER 18

Northam Bridge 1952 – 1954

The wrought iron road bridge spanning the River Itchen at Northam had been in place since 1889 (having then succeeded the original wooden structure) but by the late 1930s was deemed inadequate for the growing vehicular traffic. However, the intervention of the Second World War delayed its replacement and, with materials being in short supply in the aftermath, work did not commence until 1952.

The new bridge was built alongside its predecessor, the contract being awarded to the firm of Christiani & Nielsen Ltd who a year earlier had been engaged in the construction of new jetties at the Esso Fawley Refinery. Work at Northam commenced in April 1952 and continued until the official opening in October 1954. During this time 3,000 tons of cement and 16,000 tons of aggregate were used in the manufacture of pre-stressed concrete beams of up to 50 tons each. These were in spans of 85 to 105 feet that were manufactured in large pits over which gantries lifted them on to rail bogies for transport to a jetty. There, they were loaded upon pontoons which were fitted with shear legs, then floated out to the bridge piers and lifted into position.

During the construction works, the standard gauge tramway to the Northam Wharves was diverted from its original level crossing at the approach of the old bridge to a route that passed underneath the new one.

The contractors yard was temporarily laid over a children's playground and the rail system was a basic triangle formation, the main section of which served the beam construction pits and led out on to the jetty. The track gauge was 3 ft, the same as that employed at their previous site at Esso Refinery where several Hibberd "Planet" locomotives were used. A pair of such locomotives was also used at Northam, and it is possible these two were previously on the Fawley contract. Of the five connected with the refinery works, three are reported as sold on to other concerns afterwards but not so numbers 3454 and 3467, and these may well have been transferred to the Northam Bridge site.

As they were still quite new, both having been acquired from the makers in March 1950, it is almost certain the two locos were used on subsequent contracts before C&N was taken over by its Thai subsidiary in 1992, but no further records of the duo have yet come to hand. For further details of these locomotives, see the chapter about the Fawley Refinery on page 87.

The new bridge construction takes shape alongside the old iron bridge at the top of the photo. The contractor's railway and jetty are seen centre right. (Southampton City Archive)

Above: One of the contractor's locos is glimpsed on the extreme right of the photo, next to one of the concrete beam construction pits. (Southampton City Archive)

Opposite page, top: The general scene at Northam with the contractor's narrow gauge tracks in the centre of the photo and the standard gauge Northam Tramway in the foreground. (Southampton City Archive)

Opposite page, bottom: In a busy scene at the contractor's site, one of the locos heads a train under the furthest gantry while the other sits off rails in the middle of the photo. (Southampton City Archives)

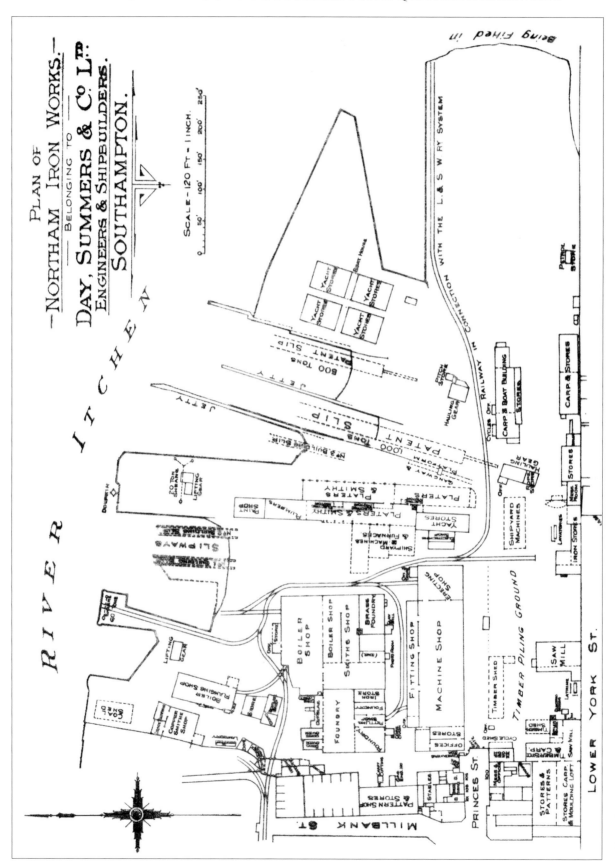

Plan of the Day, Summers & Co shipyard showing the works railway system circa 1900.

Northam Quay Tramway 1840 – 1984

A tramway from Northam Quay to the nearby coke ovens came into being around 1840 and was soon extended to connect the various industrial premises along the adjacent wharves to the main London & Southampton Railway line. The shipbuilding firm of Summers, Groves & Day (latterly Day, Summers & Co Ltd) had been set up at Northam Iron works at this time, having moved from the Millbrook Foundry (see page 49) and their new yard developed an intricate rail system that served a large collection of buildings such as foundries, boiler shops, fitting and machine shops, smithies, stores and jetties.

The motive power on the tramway was first provided by the firm of Dixon & Cardus, who employed *Eva*, a Manning Wardle saddle tank purchased in 1911, then *Nicholson*, a Fowler 0-4-2T which succeeded it from 1919. After shipbuilding on the River Itchen began to wane, Summers closed in 1929 and part of the site was taken over by ship repairers John I Thornycroft but the majority of the yard was acquired by scrap merchants Pollock, Brown & Co who continued to use the available loco.

When Dixon & Cardus closed in 1934 the operation of the line was taken over by the Le Dansk Margarine factory, and *Nicholson* was replaced by a Muir Hill petrol locomotive No L112 supplied new that year.

The route of the tramway was altered in the mid 1950s with the building of a new road bridge across the River Itchen, together with the development of the Southern Independent Television Studios. The margarine factory ceased business in 1957, following which Pollock, Brown & Co provided an alternative locomotive in the shape of a Ruston & Hornsby diesel No 305310 built in 1952. The Muir Hill engine was then taken out of service and converted to a wagon.

At the end of main line steam in the mid-1960s the Ruston could regularly be observed hauling trains of cut-up locomotives on their final journeys, appropriately at funeral pace, along the tramway to the scrapyard. A succession of other locos also saw service at the yard, but a number of these could be considered as temporary or "visitors", being used only for short periods while in transit, or seeing out the end of their working lives before joining the scrapheap themselves. Ruston 305310 remained in service until it, and the remaining locos, were broken up after closure of the tramway in 1984. The yard is currently operated by the firm of European Metal Recycling Ltd and virtually all traces of the railway have disappeared.

Ruston & Hornsby No 305310 amidships between the wagons on the section of the line that passed under Northam Bridge circa 1960. (E.S. Small)

Northam Iron Works 4wPM Muir Hill No L112

Manufacturer:	Muir Hill Engineering Ltd, Trafford Park, Manchester
Built:	1934
Works number:	L112
Engine:	Fordson
Driving Wheels:	3ft 4in
Weight:	4ton 0cwt
At Northam:	1934 – 1957

Not the most picturesque locomotive, this Muir Hill vehicle was supplied new to the Northam Tramway in 1934, replacing the former Dixon and Cardus Ltd 0-4-2T *Nicholson* which was scrapped that year. Initially it served both the Le Dansk margarine factory and the iron works, which was by then occupied by scrap merchants Pollock, Brown & Co Ltd. By 1957 it had been replaced by a small Ruston diesel (No 305310/1952) and its chassis was utilised in conversion to a wagon. This remnant survived until broken up in late 1962.

Northam Iron Works 4wDM Ruston & Hornsby No 305310

Manufacturer:	Ruston & Hornsby Ltd, Lincoln
Built:	1952
Works number:	305310
Running number:	PB 56
Engine:	48hp Ruston 48DS
Driving Wheels:	2ft 6in
Wheelbase:	5ft 2in
Weight:	6ton 0cwt
At Northam:	1957 – 1985

This small Ruston was dispatched from the makers in November 1952 and delivered new to Western Metallurgical Industries (George Cohen Ltd) at Graig Trewyddfa. Its duties there ended when transferred to Pollock Brown & Co (another subsidiary of the Cohen group) at the Northam Iron Works, replacing the previously used Muir Hill petrol loco in 1957. It became a stalwart of the Northam Tramway, remaining in service until the line closed in 1984, after which it was scrapped with others at the works.

Northam Iron Works 0-4-0DM Fowler No 4200002

Manufacturer:	John Fowler & Co (Leeds) Ltd, Hunslet, Leeds
Built:	1946
Works number:	4200002
Running number:	Yard No 243 (Royal Navy)
Engine:	150hp Fowler 4C
Driving Wheels:	3ft 3in
Wheelbase:	5ft 6in
Weight:	29ton 0cwt
At Northam:	1969 – 1983

Fowler No 4200002 was delivered new to the Admiralty in April 1946 for use at the Royal Naval Armament Depot at Dean Hill on the Hampshire-Wiltshire border, seeing service there as Yard No 243 until sold to Pollock, Brown & Co at Northam in 1969. It remained at the ironworks until scrapped in June 1983, unlike several others of the Northam fleet that had lingered until being disposed of after the tramway closed in 1984.

Muir Hill No L112 seen on the tramway sidings at Northam on 15th June 1954 when the new road bridge in the background was still under construction. (M.H. Walshaw)

Pollock, Brown & Co No 56, Ruston 305310, in its final days at Northam Ironworks on 22nd December 1984. (Bert Moody collection)

Fowler loco No 4200002 emerges from under Northam Bridge heading for the main line exchange sidings on 12th July 1975. (Bert Moody Collection)

Northam Iron Works 4wDM Ruston & Hornsby No 198306

Manufacturer:	Ruston & Hornsby Ltd, Lincoln
Built:	1940
Works number:	198306
Engine:	13hp
At Northam:	1972 – 1975

Originally built to 2ft 0in gauge, this loco was supplied new to J.R. Pratt & Son at the Chardstock Sand Quarry, near Axminster in April 1940. Having left them for an unknown destination in 1945 it was at sometime rebuilt to standard gauge before being sold to Pollock, Brown & Co at Northam in 1972. However, its unsuccessful stay there lasted for only three years before it was scrapped in 1975.

Northam Iron Works 0-4-0DM Fowler No 22996

Manufacturer:	John Fowler & Co (Leeds) Ltd, Hunslet, Leeds
Built:	1943
Works number:	22996
Running number:	PB 1001, AMW No 242 (Air Force)
Engine:	150hp Fowler 4C
Driving Wheels:	3ft 3in
Wheelbase:	6ft 3in
Weight:	25ton 0cwt
At Northam:	1972 – 1985

No 22996 was dispatched from Fowlers in April 1943 and delivered new to the Air Ministry at Carlisle. After being rebuilt by the makers it was transferred to RAF Chilmark, Wiltshire in July 1955, remaining there until sold to Pollock, Brown & Co at Northam in December 1972. There it saw service with other members of the ironworks fleet until rail operations ceased in 1984. It was subsequently broken up in March 1985.

Northam Iron Works 0-4-0DM Fowler No 22968

Manufacturer:	John Fowler & Co (Leeds) Ltd, Hunslet, Leeds
Built:	1942
Works number:	22968
Running number:	PB 1000, AMW No 221 (Air Force)
Engine:	150hp Fowler 4C
Driving Wheels:	3ft 3in
Wheelbase:	6ft 3in
Weight:	26ton 0cwt
At Northam:	1974 – 1985

Fowlers delivered No 22968 to the Air Ministry at Quedgeley near Gloucester in January 1942 where it saw service until being rebuilt by the makers and transferred to the Air Force Hartlebury maintenance depot at Worcester in February 1956. It was then at Carlisle before returning to Hartlebury in 1960. In August 1974 it was sold to George Cohen's Cransley Depot in Northants before moving on to their subsidiary, Pollock, Brown & Co at Northam a month later. There it joined another ex-service Fowler No 22996 and remained at the ironworks until the tramway closed in 1984, before being scrapped the following March.

Fowler No 22996 as Pollock, Brown's No PB 1001 at Northam Ironworks on 22nd December 1984. Its older sister, PB 1000 No 22968/1942, is behind. (Bert Moody collection)

Fowler No 22968 hauls a train of empty wagons at Drivers Wharf, heading towards the Ironworks, in the 1970s. (Bert Moody Collection)

Northam Iron Works 0-4-0DM Hunslet No 4262

Manufacturer:	Hunslet Engine Co Ltd, Hunslet, Leeds
Built:	1952
Works number:	4262
Running number:	Yard No 6952 (Navy)
Engine:	93/102hp Gardner 4L3
Driving Wheels:	3ft 4in
Wheelbase:	5ft 6in
Weight:	21ton 0cwt
At Northam:	1976 – 1985

This Hunslet loco was delivered new to Portsmouth Dockyard in February 1952, its naval service lasting until 1971 when sold to PD Fuels at Dibles Wharf in Southampton (see page 131). Its time at Dibles lasted until July 1976 when a short journey up the River Itchen saw it arrive at the Northam Ironworks of Pollock, Brown & Co. This proved to be its final duty as, after the tramway closed in 1984, it was scrapped along with the rest of the PB fleet in 1985.

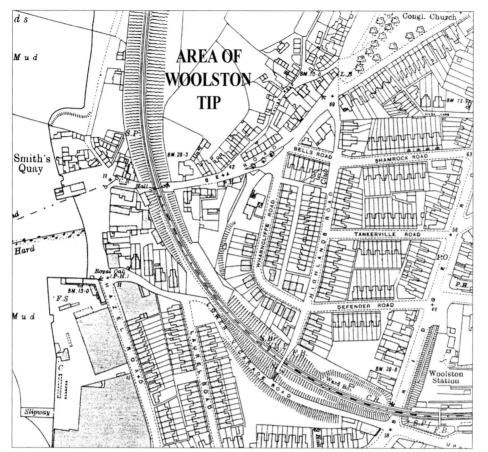

Left: This Ordnance Survey map of Woolston dates from 1933 but includes the waste area that was to become Woolston Tip. Woolston station is shown at the bottom right with the shoreline of the River Itchen down the left hand side.
(Reproduced from 1933 Ordnance Survey map with the kind permission of the Ordnance Survey.)

Below: The veteran Hunslet takes a break from Woolston and is pictured at Eastleigh in 1965 before its return.
(Jeff Pain)

Woolston Tip 1954 – 1976

This refuse tip was situated at Peartree, just to the north west of Woolston BR station, on the eastern side of the main line that overlooks, and runs alongside, the River Itchen. The area between the railway line and the habitations at Sea Road was known locally as "Donkeys Common", part of which was a deep gully between the railway embankment and the surrounding high ground, the bottom of which was littered with wild shrubs and several ponds. The local council decided that this should be filled in and, from December 1954, temporary sidings were laid and adjoined to the main line, enabling wagons laden with spoil and rubbish to be transported to the site and tipped into the infill area, the trains being operated by BR.

The site was subsequently operated by the contracting firm of R Robinson & Co (Westminster) Ltd, who employed two successive diesel shunters between 1960 and 1971. During this time, the uneven and twisted track was often moved around to afford the best vantage points for tipping and, overnight, the locomotive wheels were chained to the rails to deter the local vandals from joyriding. From 1971, operation of the rubbish trains was again taken over by BR locomotives and this arrangement continued until the tip closed in June 1976.

Ex-War Department Hunslet No 1858 photographed at Woolston tip while securely tethered one evening in 1963. (Author)

Woolston Tip 0-4-0DM Hunslet No 1858

Manufacturer:	Hunslet Engine Co Ltd, Hunslet, Leeds
Built:	1937
Works number:	1858
Running numbers:	70226, WD 811 (War Dept), 811
Engine:	40/44HP Fowler 4B
Driving Wheels:	2ft 9in
Wheelbase:	5ft 6in
Weight:	10ton 0cwt
At Woolston Tip:	1960 – 1964 and 1965 – 1969

This loco was built for the War Department, having been completed in September 1937. During its military service it saw duty at Sinfin Lane Technical Stores Depot, Derby from January 1952 until May 1959. By September that year it had moved to Longmoor where its military service ended when sold to contractors R Robinson & Co (Westminster) Ltd in February 1960. Under its new owners it was employed in the less glamorous task of dumping spoil at the Woolston tip. The tip was temporarily closed in 1964 and the loco was transferred to Eastleigh Works where it performed a similar role until returning to Woolston in April 1965. By 1969 it had been succeeded by another 0-4-0DM, in the shape of Fowler No 22288 and, being surplus to requirements, was scrapped in June the following year.

See the previous two pages for pictures of this loco.

Woolston Tip 0-4-0DM Fowler No 22288

Manufacturer:	John Fowler & Co (Leeds) Ltd, Hunslet, Leeds
Built:	1938
Works number:	22288
Engine:	40hp Sanders
Driving Wheels:	2ft 6in
Wheelbase:	5ft 6in
Weight:	10ton 0cwt
At Woolston Tip:	1969 – 1971

Fowler No 22288 was supplied new to Ashton Containers Ltd at Bristol, having been dispatched by the makers in February 1938. Its time there ended in July 1965, when sold to dealers Joseph Pugsley & Sons at Stoke Gifford, Gloucestershire; remaining with them until moving on to contractor R Robinson & Co (Westminster) Ltd at their Woolston site in 1969. There it succeeded the existing diesel veteran HE No 1858/1937 and continued to labour at the tip until being scrapped in September 1971 when BR locos took over the operation.

The second Robinson loco to work at Woolston tip was Fowler No 22288 pictured on site in 1969, still bearing the logo of its former owners Joseph Pugsley. (Jeff Pain)

CHAPTER 21

Woolston Shipyard 1876 – 1982

Almost 130 years of shipbuilding at Woolston came to an end when the yard of Vosper Thornycroft, covering some 32 acres, closed its gates in March 2004. It also marked the end of an industry on the river Itchen that had been established since the 1830s. For many years during its history the Woolston yard had its own railway connecting the various buildings and, at its peak, was quite a comprehensive network having evolved as the works developed. Although the main line came to Woolston in 1866 this purely internal railway was never connected to it.

Having moved south from Wearside, Thomas Oswald ran the yard from 1876, together with partner John Mordaunt. It is thought the embryonic works railway was laid down during around this time, and the firm of Oswald, Mordaunt & Co lasted until 1889, having produced some 104 vessels before going bust. The following year a new company rose from the ashes under the name of the Naval Iron Works, but it was short lived, lasting only until 1893 before it too went into receivership.

The yard saw no more activity until the yacht builders J.G. Fay resurrected part of it in 1897. The bulk of the yard was then taken up by Morden Carney & Co Ltd who, during their tenure from 1899 to 1904, considerably modernised by the works before selling out to John I Thornycroft in 1904. Since that time the yard saw continued growth and progress.

There has never been any evidence of locomotives working in the yard. In its early years the railway would have been worked by horses, but a number of small rail mounted steam cranes took over the movement of materials in the early Thornycroft days. In the 1950s large steel plates and other heavy loads were transported around the works on bogie wagons, and it would appear that by the 1960s only a pair of the cranes remained, with just one still being evident as late as 1982.

The rail system had considerably diminished by the 1970s when large new buildings were erected over much of the site, and the majority of the remaining track seems to have finally disappeared during the 1980s, with little or nothing left by the time of the yard's closure and its relocation to Portsmouth.

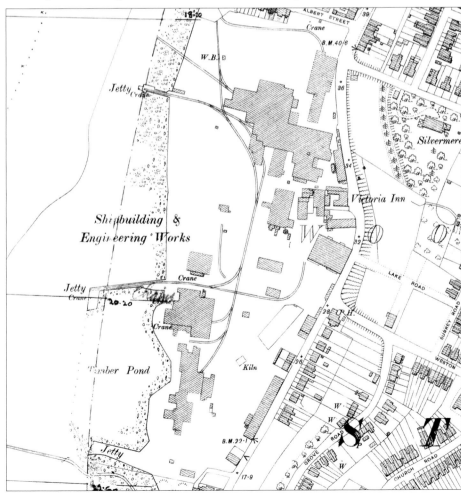

This 1897 map shows the shipyard railway covering an extensive works site which included two jetties. The foreshore appears to be beach rather than a constructed quayside.
(Reproduced from 1897 Ordnance Survey map with the kind permission of the Ordnance Survey.)

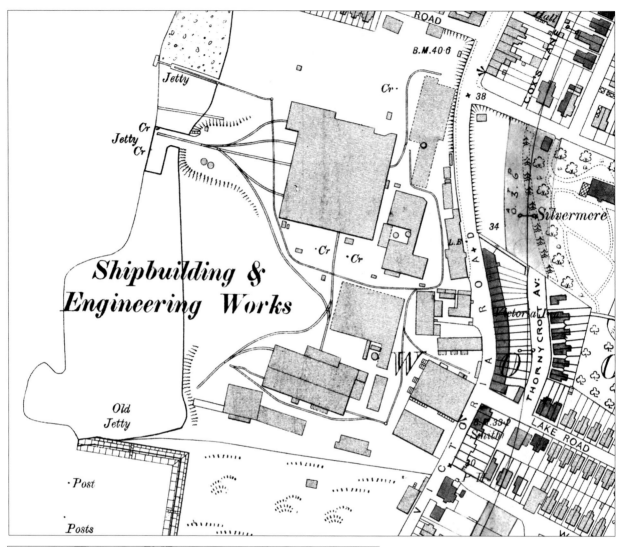

Above: By 1910 the yard reached southwards only as far as Weston Grove Road with the newer buildings now concentrated to the north of a new coal barge dock shown bottom left. (Reproduced from 1910 Ordnance Survey map with the kind permission of the Ordnance Survey.)

Left: One of the shipyard's rail mounted steam cranes assists at the steel rolling plant in the 1930s. (Author's collection)

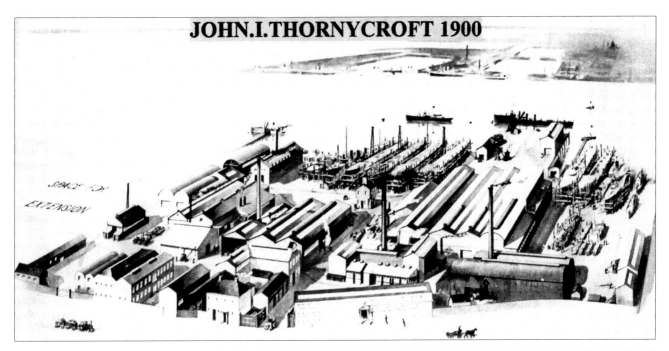

JOHN. I. THORNYCROFT 1900

Above: A turn-of-the-century representation of the Thornycroft yard shows the large spread of works and slipways – with the odd glimpse of the rail tracks and cranes, but the date is incorrect as J.I.T. did not arrive until 1904.
(Ted Wills Collection)

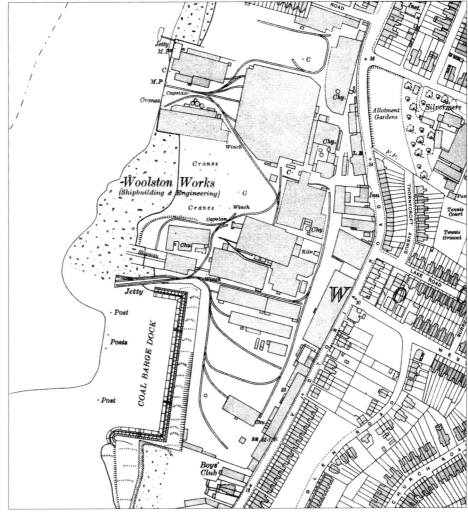

Right: By 1933 the yard had extended southwards again and occupied the ground to the rear of the coal barge dock. By now, the rail network serving the buildings around the yard was quite complex.
(Reproduced from 1933 Ordnance Survey map with the kind permission of the Ordnance Survey.)

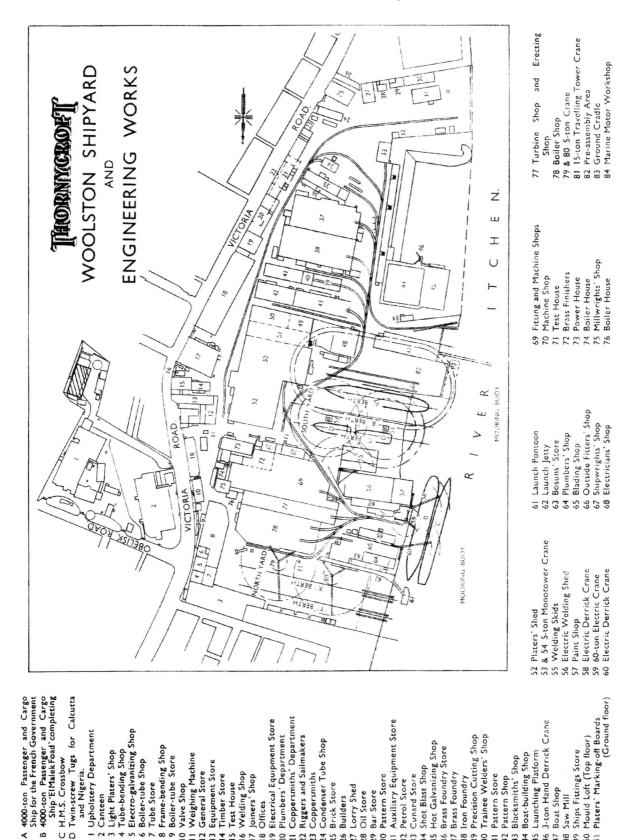

A plan of Thornycroft's Woolston Shipyard in 1947 shows the key buildings and the rail network that served them. (Author's Collection)

A 4000-ton Passenger and Cargo
    Ship for the French Government
B 4000-ton Passenger and Cargo
    Ship 'El Malek Foad' completing
C H.M.S. Crossbow
D Twin-screw Tugs for Calcutta
    and Nigeria.
1 Upholstery Department
2 Canteen
3 Light Platers' Shop
4 Tube-bending Shop
5 Electro-galvanizing Shop
6 Boiler-tube Shop
7 Tube Store
8 Frame-bending Shop
9 Boiler-tube Store
10 Valve Shop
11 Weighing Machine
12 General Store
13 Equipment Store
14 Timber Store
15 Test House
16 Welding Shop
17 Joiners' Shop
18 Offices
19 Electrical Equipment Store
20 Plumbers' Department
21 Coppersmiths' Department
22 Riggers and Sailmakers
23 Coppersmiths
24 Condenser Tube Shop
25 Brick Store
26 Builders
27 Lorry Shed
28 Oil Store
29 Bar Store
30 Pattern Store
31 Auxiliary Equipment Store
32 Petrol Store
33 Cunard Store
34 Shot Blast Shop
35 Hot Galvanizing Shop
36 Brass Foundry Store
37 Brass Foundry
38 Iron Foundry
39 Precision Cutting Shop
40 Trainee Welders' Shop
41 Pattern Store
42 Pattern Store
43 Blacksmiths' Shop
44 Boat-building Shop
45 Launching Platform
46 3-ton Hand Derrick Crane
47 Boat Shop
48 Saw Mill
49 Ships Fittings Store
50 Mould Loft (Top floor)
51 Platers' Marking-off Boards
    (Ground floor)

52 Platers' Shed
53 & 54 5-ton Monotower Crane
55 Welding Skids
56 Electric Welding Shed
57 Paint Shop
58 Electric Derrick Crane
59 60-ton Electric Crane
60 Electric Derrick Crane

61 Launch Pontoon
62 Launch Jetty
63 Bosuns' Store
64 Plumbers' Shop
65 Blading Shop
66 Outside Fitters' Shop
67 Shipwrights' Shop
68 Electricians' Shop

69 Fitting and Machine Shops
70 Machine Shop
71 Test House
72 Brass Finishers
73 Power House
74 Boiler House
75 Millwrights' Shop
76 Boiler House

77 Turbine Shop and Erecting
    Shop
78 Boiler Shop
79 & 80 5-ton Crane
81 15-ton Travelling Tower Crane
82 Pre-assembly Area
83 Ground Cradle
84 Marine Motor Workshop

CHAPTER 22

Netley Hospital Railway 1900 – 1955

Opened in 1863, at three stories high and 470 yards long, the grandiose building of Netley Hospital was a masterpiece of Victorian splendour, but whether the design was entirely suited to caring for the sick and wounded is a matter of debate. At any rate its facilities were far superior to the appalling field hospitals where casualties suffered in the Crimean War. Such was the concern at those conditions it was decided to build a hospital in the south of England for the reception and care of the unfortunate invalids.

The site at Netley was eventually chosen after several other considerations because of its proximity to Southampton Docks, where, upon landing from their sea journey, the injured troops would be transferred by boat to the hospital pier. This was a 560ft long iron construction reaching out to the deep water over the shallow foreshore.

Oddly, the first locomotives to appear at the hospital had arrived long before any railway connection, and were employed by the building contractor, a Mr Myers, as stationery engines for driving machinery. These were former passenger 2-2-0 tender locos built by Bury, Curtis & Kennedy of Liverpool in about 1859. They came on hire via engineer Isaac Watts Boulton of Ashton-under-Lyne near Stockport, having already been adapted for their purpose. At the end of the construction in 1863 they were returned to Boulton's yard where they stood unused until being broken up during the following year.

This aerial photograph shows the vast buildings of the main hospital on the foreshore and the sprawling Red Cross encampment at the rear. (Hampshire Record Office)

AMBULANCE TRAIN   *Netley LSWR*

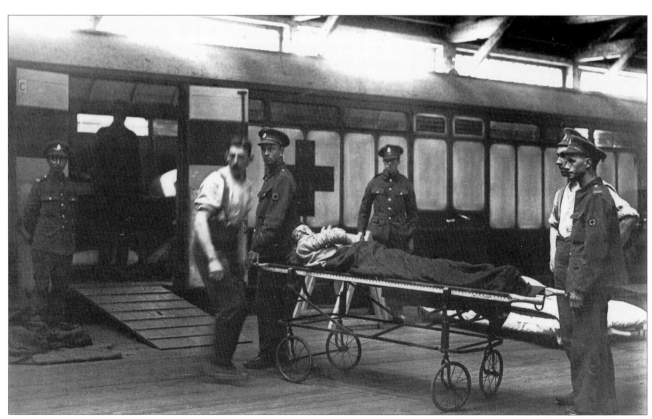

After many schemes, put forward by several railway companies, the Southampton and Netley Railway was eventually constructed in 1866 to convey the military personnel in ambulance trains direct from the docks, but in the initial years they still had to endure the indignity of being transferred the final three quarters of a mile from Netley station to the hospital by hand cart! Queen Victoria, being a frequent visitor to the hospital, was instrumental in persuading the government to fund a branch from the station to the hospital in 1900. It was built by the LSWR and terminated at a fully-covered 196-feet long platform on the north side of the hospital building. In addition to the station buildings, five ambulance coaches were housed in an adjacent corrugated shed.

During the First World War, such was the need for medical accommodation that the main buildings were supplemented by a Red Cross hospital, which consisted of dozens of huts and tents erected in the hospital grounds and

Above: LSWR 415 Class 4-4-2T loco No 170 at Netley Hospital station. (Hampshire Records Office)

Opposite page, top: 0-6-0 loco No 336 with an ambulance train at Netley LSWR Station. (Author's Collection)

Opposite page, bottom: Patient care improved considerably when trains were able to run directly to the hospital station. Here, a casualty arrives at Netley hospital in 1915. (Kidderminster Railway Museum)

swelled the bed capacity to 2500 from the original 1000.

Ambulance trains from as far as Plymouth, Avonmouth and Birkenhead brought their wounded to Netley, some of these trains being too long for the hospital platform and having to deposit their occupants in relays.

The line itself suffered from a steep gradient down to the hospital and stringent speed restrictions were necessary whilst travelling inwards. In the opposite direction, in later years the longer US Army trains required a banking engine to assist the main locomotive "up the hill".

Understandably, the number of trains was much less between the First and Second World Wars, but the new conflict from 1939 saw movements rise again as casualties mounted, and these also included numbers of American personnel. Peacetime once again saw services dwindle and maintenance trains were, by and large, the only traffic seen on the branch in post war years. Rail working finally ceased at the end of August 1955 and the hospital itself fell into disrepair following its closure in 1958, but some of the track remained in place for another 20 years.

The locomotives that worked the line were many and varied, but were usually the smaller engines of the LSWR, latterly the Southern Railway, with occasional visits by GNR J3s. Some larger types appeared during WWII such as LNER B12/3s and Southern K10s, while Brighton E1s were also employed for banking duties. A few stock movements were carried out after the war by classes such as the ageing SR S11s or BR-built class 3s.

The derelict hospital building was badly damaged in a malicious fire in 1963 and demolition began some three years later, leaving just the hospital chapel standing in the vast open grounds. These were purchased by Hampshire County Council in 1979 and opened the following year as the Royal Victoria Country Park.

Netley's main line station still welcomes travellers on the route between Portsmouth and Southampton, but none of the track to the hospital remains, and parts of the route have been built upon since closure. However, the sounds of trains are still heard in the country park as a small 10¼in gauge leisure railway currently operates there at weekends.

Discharged military personnel await their train at the Hospital Station while observing some light track maintenance. (Author's Collection)

Opposite page, bottom: A scene from the end of the railway. The tracks are gone and demolition of the hospital and its station is under way in 1966. (R.K. Blencowe Collection)

This photograph from 1952 shows the run-down appearance of the hospital in the years before closure of the branch in 1955. (Kettering Railway Museum)

S11 class Loco No 30396 on the Netley Hospital branch line on 22nd May 1950. (John A. Bailey/Bert Moody Collection)

Hamble Road Sidings 1918 – 1986

This railway ran from the LSWR main line east of Netley, from a point just west of the present Hamble station. It was originally built to serve to the Admiralty's Marine Acceptance Depot, which was constructed by contractor Trollop & Coles on the site of the present day BP oil terminal. Work began in 1917 and the rail connection was completed during the following year but the seaplane depot, as yet unfinished, was abandoned at the end of WWI. By 1919 a site to the west of the depot had passed into the hands of AV Roe and Co Ltd, who operated an aeroplane factory and airfield (Hamble South). They built their own connection to the line from a point just south of Hamble Lane, their siding being used for the movement of aircraft parts, stores and coal. During the construction of the aerodrome, by contractor Sir Lindsay Parkinson & Co, a two-foot gauge railway was engaged in the site works and operated by a Kerr, Stuart 0-4-2ST loco (No 3051/1918).

Roe were sole users of the line until the derelict Marine Depot was taken over by Shell Mex in 1923. An oil terminal with a pier had been constructed by the following year. Until that time, the line had been operated by on-loan locomotives from the LSWR, one being the former Southampton Dock Company engine *Clausentum*. Shell initially worked their terminal system with horses hired from nearby farms but, by 1926, had taken delivery of their first locomotive, an Avonside 0-6-0ST No 1820 of 1919, This had come from the War Department Depot at Bramley and was allocated the running number 5.

By 1928, a 4-wheel petrol loco (SM&BP No 7) had arrived, and a new airfield, to the north of Hamble Lane, had been laid out by 1931 (although this entailed planes having to cross the railway to reach the hangars). By 1934, AV Roe ceased operations, being replaced by the firm of Air Service Training Ltd (and eventually Petters). They soon extended their factory and built over the existing works rails, but added an engine shed and a new siding to the north of their plant. The shed was located near the present day rail crossing at Baron Road and housed the Avonside loco.

During WWII, the factories at Hamble were understandably very busy repairing and overhauling Spitfires, with a workforce hailing from as far as Dorset and Sussex. In 1941 there was a proposal to run passenger

Hudswell Clarke D707 as SM&BP No 21 heads a train to the exchange sidings on 2nd March 1963. (Roger Holmes)

trains along the Hamble railway to save personnel the long walk to and from the nearest station at Netley. This was turned down, but Hamble Halt was built by January the following year and a bus service established from there. Also, in 1942, the increase in Ministry of Supply traffic had led to a third loop being added to the dual sidings at the junction with the main line.

Loco No 7 had been replaced in 1937 by No 13, a 4-wheel diesel mechanical engine, delivered new from makers FC Hibberd bearing the works number 2012. The duties of both numbers 7 and 13 had been mainly confined to the localities of the terminal, while No 5 operated the section up to the main line. A Hudswell Clarke 0-6-0 diesel (D707) was delivered new in April 1950 – more power being needed at that time after the line had been upgraded to take heavier trains.

By June that year, the redundant No 5 had been dispatched to the Hunslet Engine Co at Leeds, and was soon followed out of Hamble by No 13, which was transferred by road to the company's Purfleet depot in September that year. This removal happened after the arrival of No 18, a Fowler 0-4-0 diesel (No 22973/1942) a month earlier.

The Hudswell Clarke loco took the running number 21 and worked on until 1967 when it was replaced by new Hunslet 0-6-0 diesel No 6950 (No 24), and was handed over to the Mid Hants Railway. No 24 became the last of the Hamble locos, working on until rail traffic all but ceased in 1985, after which the loco was placed in store and finally sent the company's depot at the Isle of Grain.

However that was not quite the end of the railway. During the months of August to December in 1985, evaluation trials were carried out on trains between the oil

This railway scene at the Hamble Depot shows No 24 at rest in the loco shed. (J.R. Fairman)

wells at Wytch Farm in Dorset and the terminal at Hamble, with movements at the Hamble end being worked by BR locos and class 08 shunters on a weekly rotation.

Commercial rail traffic officially ended in 1986 but the oil terminal also had a separate narrow gauge line that ran the length of the pier. This was used for ships stores and worked by hand propelled wagons until 1966 when a double bogie battery electric loco was purchased new from Greenwood & Batley (No 6132) to operate the 1ft 8in gauge line. The loco was housed in a small shed at the landward end of the pier. It appears that this system, and the locomotive, was discarded during a major refurbishment of the jetty in 1988 which enabled larger tankers to dock for the Wytch Farm crude oil.

With the closure of the rail link, supplies were brought in by sea tankers, this arrangement continuing until a pipeline was completed to carry the crude oil from Dorset to Hamble in 1990. Since rail operations ceased, a number of enthusiasts' specials have been the only movements on the line.

Finally, a mystery loco appeared on the scene towards the end of November in 1992. This was named *Man of Kent* and had been transferred from BP's recently closed installation at the Isle of Grain. It was a Thomas Hill 0-6-0DH No 294V having been built in 1981. During 1993 it was given a new livery and renamed *Hamble-le-Rice* but never ventured outside the oil terminal gates before being transferred to Coryton in October 1998.

To date, the Hamble Road Sidings remain mostly intact should the need for a rail link ever return, and the route of the railway now forms part of a woodland walk sponsored by owners BP Oil.

Hamble Oil Terminal and jetty as seen from the air. (Associated British Ports)

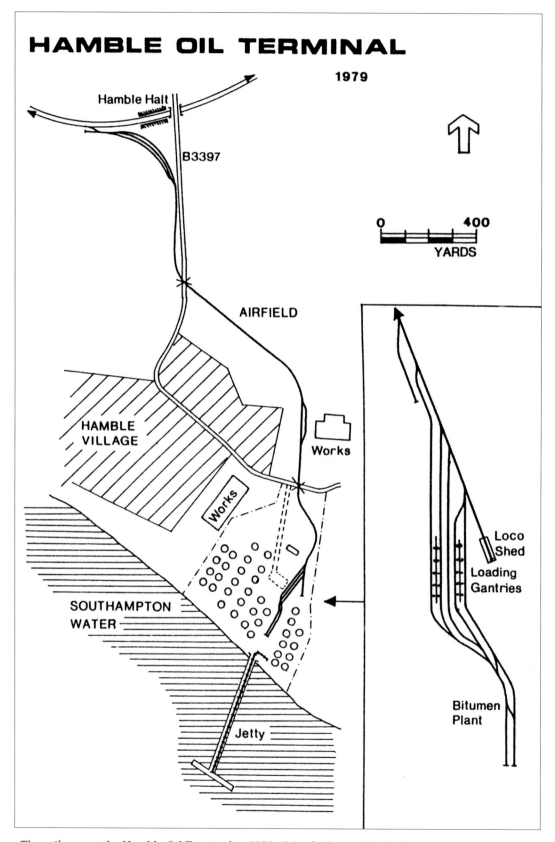

HAMBLE OIL TERMINAL

1979

Hamble Halt

B3397

AIRFIELD

HAMBLE VILLAGE

Works

Works

SOUTHAMPTON WATER

Jetty

0   400
YARDS

Loco Shed

Loading Gantries

Bitumen Plant

The railways at the Hamble Oil Terminal in 1979. (Map by Roger Hateley)

Shell Mex & BP No 5 0-6-0ST Avonside No 1820

Name:	*(Bramley No 7)*
Manufacturer:	Avonside Engine Co Ltd, Fishponds Works, Bristol
Built:	1919
Works number:	1820
Running numbers:	7 (WD Bramley), 5 (SM&BP)
Cylinders:	14.5in x 20in
Driving wheels:	3ft 3in
Wheelbase:	9ft 8.5in
Weight:	35ton 0cw
At Hamble:	1926 – 1946 & 1950

Avonside No 1820 was delivered new to the War Department army depot at Bramley in 1919 where it took the name *Bramley No 7* until it was sold to Shell Mex & BP at Hamble in February 1926. While engaged on the Oil Terminal traffic this loco also worked trains to the adjacent AV Roe aeroplane works. During 1946 it was transferred to Shell's depot at Lymington for four years until moving back to Hamble in June 1950. However, its return was short-lived. Having been replaced by a diesel (Hudswell Clarke D707/1950), it was now surplus to requirements, and on the 22nd of that month it was dispatched by rail *en route* to the Hunslet Engine Co at Leeds (who had taken over Avonside in 1935), but it ran hot bearings on the journey and was held over at Eastleigh for a spell of attention. After reaching Hunslet it was on hire to the National Coal Board at their Rothwell Colliery, near Leeds in December 1951 and subsequently purchased by them before moving to Shaw Cross Colliery, at Osset, near Wakefield, around 1958, working there for the remainder of its time until scrapped in February 1961.

Shell Mex & BP No 5, Avonside 0-6-0ST No 1820/1919, at Hamble Oil Terminal on 17th May 1950. (John A. Bailey/Bert Moody Collection)

Hamble Aerodrome 0-4-2ST Kerr, Stuart No 3051

Manufacturer:	Kerr, Stuart & Co Ltd, California Works, Stoke on Trent
Built:	1918
Works number:	3051
Cylinders:	7in x 12in
Driving wheels:	2ft 0in
Wheelbase:	3ft 0in
Weight:	8ton 10cwt
Gauge:	2ft 0in
At Hamble:	1918 – 1919

This Kerr, Stuart "Tattoo" class narrow gauge loco was employed by contractor Sir Lindsay Parkinson during the building of Hamble (South) Aerodrome for A.V. Roe & Co, having been delivered new in June 1918 via the Ministry of Munitions. It worked until completion of the airfield in 1919 after which it is thought to have moved to T.W. Ward at Grays before returning to Parkinson in July 1929 for the construction of their East Lancashire Road contract, which was completed in 1934. Nothing further is recorded.

Shell Mex & BP No 7 4wPM Hibberd

Manufacturer:	F.C. Hibberd & Co Ltd, Park Royal, London
Built:	Unknown
Works number:	Unknown
Running number:	7 (SM&BP)
Engine:	40hp
At Hamble:	1928 – 1937

The identity of this locomotive is a real mystery, as is the exact period of time it spent at Hamble. It is generally thought to have been a Hibberd "Planet" loco, originally built as narrow gauge but later adapted for standard rails. It was recorded as being at Hamble in 1928 and may have been disposed of when another Hibberd loco (No 2102) arrived in 1937, but a different report suggests it was still there in a disused state in 1948 and was finally taken away by road around August 1950, presumably for scrap.

Shell Mex & BP No 13 4wDM Hibberd No 2102

Manufacturer:	F.C. Hibberd & Co Ltd, Park Royal, London
Built:	1937
Works number:	2102
Running number:	13 (SM&BP)
Engine:	70hp Paxman Ricardo
Driving Wheels:	3ft 0in
Weight:	18ton 9cwt
At Hamble:	1937 – 1950

This "Planet" loco was completed at Hibberd's works in 1937 and delivered new to Hamble, where it was mostly employed around the oil terminal sidings, but presumably took over duties from the Avonside 0-6-0ST when that engine was taken off to Lymington. With the arrival of heavier trains in 1950, a more powerful loco was needed and, following the appearance of Fowler No 22973 in August of that year, No 2102 was dispatched a month later by road to Shell's Purfleet depot. Its stay in Essex lasted less than two years, as by February 1952 it had been moved on to the company's Trafford Park depot in Lancashire. It was then purchased in 1957 by dealers Cox & Danks who in turn sold it to Broom & Wade Ltd for use at their High Wycombe works, remaining there until rail operation ceased in March 1976. After being in store for two years it was donated by the owners to the Quainton Railway Society in August 1978 where it now awaits restoration.

Not the Hamble Aerodrome loco but this illustration shows a typical "Tattoo" class Kerr, Stewart design.
(Author's Collection)

This poor quality, but interesting photo offers a rare glimpse of Shell No 7, nearest the camera. In the background is Avonside loco No 5.
(A. Sedgwick Collection)

Shell's No 13 (Hibberd No 2102) seen here in immaculate ex-works condition in 1937.
(A. Sedgwick Collection)

Shell Mex & BP No 18 0-4-0DM Fowler No 22973

Manufacturer:	John Fowler & Co (Leeds), Hunslet. Yorks
Built:	1942
Works number:	22973
Running number:	18 (SM&BP)
Driving Wheels:	3ft 3in
Wheelbase:	6ft 3in
Engine:	150hp Fowler 4c
Weight:	29ton 0cwt
At Hamble:	1950 – 1971

Fowler No 22973 was completed for the War Department in March 1942 and delivered new to the Royal Ordnance Factory at Tamebridge, Walsall. At the end of hostilities, was sold to Shell's Purfleet depot where it worked until transfer to Hamble in August 1950, via overhaul at the manufacturer's workshops. Its arrival at Hamble saw the demise of the, by then inadequate, Hibberd loco No 2012, which went off in the opposite direction a month later. No 22973 appears to have fallen out of use following the arrival of Hunslet No 6950 in 1967 and nothing more is recorded until it was sold to M Sait of West Moors, Dorset in May 1971 and scrapped the following month.

Shell Mex & BP No 21 0-6-0DM Hudswell Clarke No D707

Manufacturer:	Hudswell Clarke and Co Ltd, Railway Foundry, Leeds
Built:	1950
Works number:	D707
Running number:	21 (SM&BP)
Engine:	204hp Gardner 8L3
Driving Wheels:	3ft 1in
Wheelbase:	8ft 0in
Weight:	32ton 0cwt
At Hamble:	1950 – 1984

D707 left the makers for Hamble in April 1950, arriving new as a replacement for Avonside 0-6-0ST No 5. At the same time it took the place of Hibberd No 13, which left a few months later due to the line having been upgraded and the heavier tank wagons needing more pulling power. After many years of admirable service, it was eventually joined by Hunslet No 6950 in 1967 and worked on until put into storage in 1983. It was presented to the Mid Hants Railway in November 1984 before eventually moving on to the South Yorkshire Railway Preservation Society around 1986 and then on to the Rutland Railway Museum at Cottesmore. Its stay there lasted until April 2007 when its latest move was to the Yaxham Light Railway in Norfolk where it awaits restoration.

Shell Mex & BP No 24 0-6-0DH Hunslet No 6950

Manufacturer:	Hunslet Engine Co Ltd, Hunslet, Leeds
Built:	1967
Works number:	6950
Running number:	24 (BP)
Engine:	325hp R-R C8SFL
Driving Wheels:	3ft 9in
Wheelbase:	9ft 6in
Weight:	55ton 0cwt
At Hamble:	1967 – 1989

The largest and most powerful of the Hamble locomotives arrived new, having been completed at the maker's works in August 1967. It did not receive its running number until being painted in BP livery in 1972 and became the last dedicated Oil Terminal loco to work the Hamble Road Sidings until the line closed at the end of 1985. After being in store for a while, it was transferred to BP's Isle of Grain Depot in April 1989 and subsequently to the Mobil Coryton Refinery in Essex. Its employment there was spasmodic and, after an overhaul at BP's loco works during 2005/2006, it was donated for preservation at the Elsecar Railway, near Barnsley, where it carries the name *Louise.*

Ex-WD Fowler No 22973 seen working at Hamble on 19th March 1959. (I.J. Bovey)

No 21 at pictured at the Hamble depot loco shed on 14th March 1959. (I.J. Bovey)

Hunslet No 6950 on the Hamble Railway in 1978. (A. Sedgwick Collection)

Shell Mex & BP 2-2+4BE Railcar Greenwood & Batley No 6132

Manufacturer:	Greenwood & Batley, Leeds
Built:	1966
Works number:	6132
Driving Wheels:	1ft 4in
Motor:	2hp
Gauge:	1ft 8in
At Hamble:	1966 – 1990

Officially described as a "Special Purpose Rail Vehicle" this Greenwood & Batley battery electric railcar was delivered in March 1966 for the purpose of carrying personnel, stores and equipment along the straight run of track, which ran the length of the oil terminal jetty. Its enclosed cab was designed to hold the driver and two passengers whilst the open rear platform could carry loads of up to one ton at a top speed of 8mph. After becoming surplus to requirements in 1988 it was eventually taken into preservation by the Hampshire Narrow Gauge Society in July 1990, and thence through several more owners before arriving at its current home in rural Norfolk where it is in need of substantial renovation.

BP's "unique" Hamble Jetty transportation vehicle as built in 1966 from an official works photo. (IRS Collection)

Shell Mex & BP 0-6-0DH Thomas Hill No 294V

Name:	*Hamble-le-Rice (Man of Kent)*
Manufacturer:	Thomas Hill (Rotherham) Ltd, Kilnhurst, Yorks
Built:	1981
Works number:	294V
Engine:	427hp Rolls-Royce DV8N
Driving Wheels:	3ft 3in
Weight:	60ton 0cwt
At Hamble:	1992 – 1998

This Thomas Hill "Vanguard" loco was supplied new to the BP Oil refinery at the Isle of Grain in Kent in 1981 and given the name *Man of Kent*. When the depot closed in 1992 this relatively new, but redundant engine, was sent to Hamble for "safe keeping" while its future was decided – even though the rail system there had been out of use since 1985. In the following year it was given a repaint and a new name, *Hamble-le-Rice,* was applied in March 1993, then, after being held in storage for some years in its new guise, it was finally sent off in October 1998 to BP's Coryton Bulk Terminal at Stanford-le-Hope in Essex, which was subsequently purchased in June 2007 by Petroplus Refining and Marketing Ltd.